JOURNEY
TO OUTSTANDING

The three key leadership strategies
for creating a truly outstanding school

JOURNEY TO OUTSTANDING:

The three key leadership strategies for creating a truly outstanding school
By Sonia Gill

Education | Leadership | Head Teacher Training | Management

First published in 2015

Writing Matters Publishing
10 Lovelace Court
Bethersden Kent UK TN26 3AY

info@writingmatterspublishing.com
www.writingmatterspublishing.com

Cover Illustration by Dale Wylie represented by Lipstick of London Ltd.

ISBN 978-0-9575440-4-8

Please Note: This book is intended as information only and does not constitute legal, financial or specific professional advice unique to your situation. The Author, Publisher and Resellers accept no responsibility for loss, damage or injury to persons or their belongings as a direct or indirect result of reading this book.

DEDICATION

I dedicate this book to those people who strive,
every day, to support, educate and care for our
children; those who challenge themselves to give
more; and those who have a relentless desire
to give the skills, knowledge, love and support,
which will let today's children go on to create
a better world and live their dreams.

Thank You

I'd like to say a heartfelt thank you to the many people who have helped me with this book. Thank you to Rebecca Harris, Am Rai, Tara Baig, Paul Robinson and Kirsten Cooper for their time and feedback in reviewing this book and Tracy Kilkenny and her senior leadership team (SLT) for their contribution.

I am grateful to the many Heads and schools I have worked with over the years and while there are too many individuals to thank by name here, I'd like to acknowledge the inspiration, challenges and improvements they have made to my work, skills and knowledge.

Thank you to *Team Heads Up* for all your hard work and commitment to making a difference and for being there for me and each other: Shiraz, Sheila, Heather, Robert, Sophie, Lucy, Emma, Amy and Kay.

A big thank you to those people who irrevocably changed my life for the better: Nick Bolton, for getting me started on my journey and being there for me every step of the way; Mel White, you've been through it all with me; Daniel Priestley, Andrew Priestley, Darshana and Marcus Ubl for helping me know why I'm here and Susie and Rod for your great advice, support, time and humour – you keep life sparkling!

In my personal life I am grateful to those who have been by my side during life's ups and downs and without whom life would be a lot harder and a lot less fun!

My family, my wonderful mum, for giving me more than any child could have hoped for and my dad, bless his soul, for his high standards and love.

My big sister Sim who picks me up and keeps me on track and her husband Kevin who tells me so much yet says so little. And Izzy and Ally who teach me life's most valuable lessons and giggle all the way through it!

Two of my best friends: Lee, one of the wisest and most giving people I have ever met; and John, for your endless help, intellect, support and laughter – you guys keep it all real.

Most of all, thank you my dearest Phil, for your unwavering support, love and guidance through thick and thin – you are my rock.

Sonia

Sonia Gill

Testimonials

Sonia Gill is an exceptionally talented business leader as well as having experience as a successful teacher. One of the factors contributing to our school's high success has been working in close partnership with *Heads Up* to establish or consolidate the processes of high quality leadership as well as other aspects of school improvement.

Sonia Gill's book *Journey to Outstanding* is a great guide for any school practitioner and leader who is aspiring to create an outstanding school. The book provides a balance of achievable practical strategies with sound theoretical evidence which are such essential factors in achieving outstanding outcomes and impact in any successful school.

Tara Baig
Outstanding Head Teacher,
Miles Coverdale Primary School,
Hammersmith and Fulham,
National Leader of Education

Sonia's book *Journey to Outstanding* is an excellent guide for all leaders of learning. She outlines her ideas for core leadership skills and values in a way that is relevant, inspiring, accessible and practical. The ideas are based on sound theory and practical evidence making this book a must for any leader aspiring to create an outstanding school.

Kirsten Cooper (Mrs)
Outstanding Head Teacher,
Nelmes Primary School, Havering

Sonia Gill has crafted a refreshing book that will appeal to aspiring, new and ambitious head teachers. She has framed the complexities of this important role alongside the realities that exist in many schools, and ensured a relevance for those that are committed to continuous improvement. Head teachers of outstanding schools will also welcome this book as it makes a contribution to an analysis of what is required for longer term sustainability and development. Local Authorities, Academy Trusts and Governing Bodies should ensure that *Journey to Outstanding* is included in every induction package for newly appointed head teachers.

Am Rai
Outstanding Head Teacher,
Montpelier School, Ealing

Great leadership is not about overnight success.
Great leadership takes practice, difficult conversations and applying the right consistent approach.
Great leadership takes courage and is helped on its journey by tailored support from a great coach like Sonia.

I love this little book. Sonia explains difficult concepts in a simple way. She demystifies all the jargon around visions and missions, so for the first time ever, I really understand the difference between the two. There are some fantastic ideas for inset days as well.

Rebecca Harris
Outstanding Head Teacher,
St George the Martyr Primary School, Camden

Contents

Introduction

Hello, I'm Sonia Gill, the Founder and Director of *Heads Up*, and we specialise in helping primary schools become outstanding.

My mission is to make every primary school in the UK outstanding; yes, in terms of the *Office for Standards in Education, Children's Services and Skills* (Ofsted), but also in being centres of excellence in all of our communities.

I'm a qualified teacher, trained in Key Stage 2, but I've taught every age from reception to year 11 (if you've ever taught reception I think you're amazing because that's the toughest year in my opinion). I had planned to go into educational psychology (that's my degree) but after some changes to the profession I decided not to, which meant, to be honest I didn't know what I wanted to be when I grew up! I sought to broaden my experience to help me find out what I liked and was fortunate to be selected for the prestigious *John Lewis Graduate Leadership Programme*.

Throughout my time there I learnt a lot; I found my focus on leadership and creating great teams combined with my passion for psychology and my skills as a class teacher led me to be successful in business. Within three years I found myself on the steering group, reporting directly to the MD, of the second largest store. Don't let me lead you on though, I made a lot of mistakes and learnt a lot of lessons!

It's funny because I think there's often the view that the public sector should learn from the business sector, but not so much the other way around. Maybe people think that businesses are more successful? I don't think they are. A lot of businesses are average. Excellence is a rare breed in any sector or industry. I think the lessons run both ways. What I learnt as a teacher was invaluable when I moved into business and, when I moved back to the public sector, the same was true.

I always wanted to return to education because to me it's the most important part of society and so *Heads Up* was born. Using the best from business with the best of education to support those who want to create great schools, *Heads Up* is all about supporting our educational leaders to create the outstanding school they have always wanted to lead.

In this book I want to share with you the insights I've found over the years and the approach and methods I've used to support hundreds school leaders create the amazing school they dream of. I hope you find it useful, I hope you enjoy it and most of all I hope you feel empowered to create the outstanding school, the centre of excellence, you have always dreamt of leading.

Sonia Gill (2015)

Section 1
There is a magic ingredient
to becoming outstanding

Chapter One

Every school can be outstanding

'Your playing small doesn't change the world."
Marianne Williamson, Return to Love

In this chapter:
- *Being truly outstanding is more than the Ofsted criteria*
- *The excuses we make for not being outstanding*
- *Any school can be outstanding regardless of its post code and demographics*
- *Good is the enemy of great*

Every school can be outstanding. What is your reaction to that statement?

Some Heads will agree, some will disagree, some will be unsure. What do you think? I truly believe this and I'm going to explain why.

I believe every school in the UK can be outstanding by creating a culture of excellence through brilliant leadership. I think you want to be a dynamic leader and you're looking for ways to do that; that's why you are reading this book. In my opinion the *desire* to improve your own leadership is one sign of a great leader.

BEING TRULY OUTSTANDING IS MORE THAN OFSTED'S CRITERIA

I need to explain what I mean by 'outstanding'. Ofsted has its criteria for being *Outstanding,* which changes and evolves, but it is one of the markers for a great school.

I've worked in a lot of schools, with a lot of Heads and a lot of senior leaders, hundreds, and what is clear to me is that we share the view that just achieving Ofsted's definition of *outstanding* is not enough.

What I have found is that Head teachers want something more than what Ofsted want and I encapsulate this in the phrase: create the school you have always dreamt of leading.

The school you have always dreamt of leading

You became a head teacher for a reason and it's unlikely to have been purely for the money or status of the job. If you did the chances are you quickly figured out that these didn't really correlate with the demands put on you.

More likely you became a head teacher to make a difference, to take the impact you had in the classroom as a teacher, across subject areas as a subject leader, across the school as a deputy head, and to another level as a Head. A level where you could create a stimulating educational environment for children, where they could achieve academically and holistically, preparing and equipping them for life, nurturing their skills and ambitions, growing their creative talents, their love for learning, their moral and cultural development and all while enjoying the fun of school, the school which you lead. I also believe you want to be outstanding both in Ofsted's eyes and your own, because I think to have become a Head you're not someone who wanted to be average – I don't think you could have become a Head if you were.

One Head described her dream school beautifully as two halves of an apple, one side being the formal academic achievement and the other being the multitude of life skills that are not measured but are nonetheless incredibly important.

Tests, tests and more tests!

And of course in your dream school you do want children to be literate and numerate and you will want good test results - I've not met a Head who isn't interested in their end of year test results which they want, and let's be honest, need, to be excellent.

But like I've said every Head I've been lucky enough to work with has also wanted to grow and develop the whole child as there is more to education than just test results.

In the summer of 2014 we saw a wonderful example of this desire to give our children more than just tests results in the touching letter from the Head of Barrowford School in Nelson, Lancashire, Rachel Tomlinson, which was inspired from a blog post by US teacher Kimberly Hurd Horst:

Please find enclosed your end of KS2 test results. We are very proud of you as you demonstrated huge amounts of commitment and tried your very best during this tricky week. However, we are concerned that these tests do not always assess all of what it is that make each of you special and unique. The people who create these tests and score them do not know each of you- the way your teachers do, the way I hope to, and certainly not the way your families do.

They do not know that many of you speak two languages. They do not know that you can play a musical instrument or that you can dance or paint a picture. They do not know that your friends count on you to be there for them or that your laughter can brighten the dreariest day.

They do not know that you write poetry or songs, play or participate in sports, wonder about the future, or that sometimes you take care of your little brother or sister after school.

They do not know that you have travelled to a really neat place or that you know how to tell a great story or that you really love spending time with special family members and friends.

They do not know that you can be trustworthy, kind or thoughtful, and that you try, every day, to be your very best... the scores you get will tell you something, but they will not tell you everything.

So enjoy your results and be very proud of these but remember there are many ways of being smart.

We both know that poor test results put pressure on you and your school and no Head's dream school has children who are illiterate or innumerate.

What do I mean by outstanding?

When I'm referring to being *outstanding* I'm referring to this kind of school, the one many Heads have spoken to me about, the school they have dreamt of and long to create. It includes what Ofsted are looking for and all those areas Heads want for their children - it's what most teachers and parents want for children - passion, skills, social and emotional well-being, fun and so much more.

I'll refer to being great, the pursuit of excellence, high performance, exceptional and more superlatives all of which are about creating that outstanding school, that picture of success: the school you have always dreamt of creating.

THERE ARE MANY REASONS (AKA EXCUSES!)

There are many reasons why people say schools can't become outstanding and I'm sure you've heard them all (and then some!) at some point or other. They usually centre around three areas:

Issue area	Supposed problem	Supposed ideal
Children	'It's the demographic of this school' Socio-economic background Free school meals Special Educational Needs (SEN) English as an Additional Language (EAL)	If these children were all tutored, if we had less on free school meals, low SEN and low EAL
Staff	'It's the staff we have in this school, they don't perform well enough'	All teachers and staff are good or better
Money	'We don't have enough money, resources, teachers, teaching assistants (TAs).'	We have a surplus every year to spend on what we want for the school

However there are schools with one, or usually several of these factors in place, who are outstanding.

WHY LEADERSHIP IS THE DIFFERENCE BETWEEN GOOD AND OUTSTANDING SCHOOLS

Outstanding schools despite the odds

You can find schools who don't have any of the supposed 'ideals', or certainly don't have all of them, but have achieved excellence.

Every year we host our annual *Heads Up* conference of recently outstanding Heads who share *Best Practice* and we purposely choose schools whose demographics are challenging, because I believe if they can do it the rest of us can.

I've had the privilege of working and interviewing many of these outstanding Head teachers and I'd like to take a moment to look at three of these schools to illustrate my point that every school can be outstanding, regardless of their context, and pick some highlights to show what it is they did to create success (to share everything they have told me would be another book!).

Paul Robinson, Woodmansterne Primary School, Lambeth, Outstanding 2013

Paul joined the school as Deputy Head teacher in September 2009 and the school was judged as *Good* in June 2010. He took up substantive Head teacher in September 2010 and was judged as *Outstanding* in November 2013.

I first met Paul as a delegate at a *Heads Up Conference*, during one of the workshop sessions.

He stood out to me because of his comments about staff development. He had a clear process in place which meant he was very focused on developing staff to improve school performance.

He believed his approach was already used by most, if not all, Heads because it seemed so logical and natural to him. I knew it wasn't widely used, not because Heads don't believe in the value of developing staff (because they do) but because I know most schools don't have such a thorough process as his, which was integrated with his *School Improvement Plan* (SIP).

He invests in the development of his whole team, but only where that development links directly to the SIP; even free training is not given if it doesn't link to the SIP because it's a distraction to what needs to be done to move the school forward. Paul says:

'I spend around £2 million of my budget on staff costs every year and so I'm not going to worry about spending £60k on Continuing Professional Development (CPD) on my team to develop them, which is double last year's CPD budget. That is only around three percent of their salary costs. If you want to get the best from your team, you need to invest in high quality, targeted and needs led professional development for the extended team – including the Premises Team!'

The school:
- Is a larger-than-average sized primary school.
- Has a higher than national average proportion of disabled pupils and those with special educational needs supported through school action.

- A higher than national average proportion of pupils from minority ethnic backgrounds many of whom speak English as an additional language.

Here is a taste of what Ofsted said:
- Pupils achieve exceptionally well. They make outstanding progress from low starting points to reach standards in reading, writing and mathematics that are significantly above average by the end of Year 6.
- Teaching is outstanding. Pupils are highly motivated in lessons because tasks and explanations are matched exceptionally well to their needs.
- Teachers are exceptionally well supported to improve their practice because leaders invest a lot of time and effort into providing bespoke training opportunities.
- The high quality of leadership from the Head teacher, his senior team and Governors has driven improvements year on year since the previous inspection so that all areas of the school's work including teaching and achievement are now outstanding.

(Ofsted inspection report, Woodmansterne 2013)

Tara Baig, Miles Coverdale Primary School, Shepherd's Bush, Outstanding 2013

Tara Baig, Head teacher of Miles Coverdale Primary School, moved her school from satisfactory to outstanding in three years. Amongst the factors that led to the school's success was the development of the school's middle leaders which Tara quickly identified as a critical area to improve.

The school:
- Is an average-sized primary school.
- Has almost three times the national average proportion of pupils supported through school action plus or with a statement of special educational.
- Has a much higher than national average proportion of pupils eligible for the pupil premium.
- Has many pupils are from minority ethnic backgrounds, with 13 different groups represented in varying proportions.
- Has over two thirds of pupils who speak English as an additional language, much higher than the national average.

Here is a taste of what Ofsted said:
- Leaders at all levels are highly ambitious for the school and all its pupils. They work closely
- together to provide an educational experience that results in pupils being exceptionally well prepared for moving on to secondary school.
- High expectations and an intolerance of mediocrity drive staff to do their very best to ensure that all pupils make outstanding progress from starting points that are generally low.
- Standards in reading, writing and mathematics at the end of Key Stage 2 have been significantly above average for the last three years.
- Pupils' attitudes to learning are exemplary. This is a school where everybody talks about learning.

- The school has an outstanding programme for promoting pupils' spiritual, moral, social and cultural development. As a result, pupils are highly respectful towards each other and members of the wider community.

(Ofsted inspection report, Miles Coverdale, 2013)

Rebecca Harris, St George the Martyr Primary School, Camden, Outstanding November 2013

The children Rebecca and her team serve often enter below age related expectation and leave above national expectation.

Having joined the school in 2010 as Head teacher, Rebecca has created an outstanding school culture with high expectations of children.

She has reduced unnecessary disruptions and distractions so that the school can focus on its primary task of teaching.

To support this she has an effective system in place which developed the quality of teaching in her school from 88% good or better and 20% outstanding in 2010 to 100% good and 88% outstanding in 2013.

To make sure her teachers can achieve this high performance Rebecca invests in her senior leaders so they can support this exceptional level of teaching and learning.

The school:
- An inner city school in central London.
- Has almost double the national average proportion of pupils supported by pupil premium.
- Has an above national average proportion of pupils from minority ethnic groups with the highest proportion being of Bangladeshi heritage.
- Has an above national average of pupils supported by school action plus or with a statement of special educational needs.

Here is a taste of what Ofsted said:
- Parents, staff and pupils say unreservedly how much they enjoy the school. They feel that teaching is of a high standard, pupils are well cared for, and the school is well led and managed.
- Pupils' achievement is outstanding. Pupils start school with low skills and experience. By the end of Year 6 attainment is above the national average.
- All pupils make at least good, or outstanding progress. This includes pupils eligible for pupil premium, with additional needs, and those of Bangladeshi heritage.
- Teachers work hard to plan and teach high quality lessons which excite, interest and enable pupils to fulfil their potential.
- The school is led exceptionally well by the Head and Deputy Head teachers.
- All leaders expect the best for every child.
- The school promotes pupils' spiritual, moral, social and cultural development outstandingly well.

(Ofsted inspection report, St George the Martyr, 2013)

I hope these examples inspire you, I think they can also be daunting because they are quite exceptional. But I do believe if these schools can be outstanding, without having the ideal conditions of perfectly rounded children who all speak English, ideal staff and excess cash in their budget, we have to ask ourselves: why can't all schools? I believe they can.

GOOD IS THE ENEMY OF GREAT

If there is one book I would make mandatory for all leaders it would be *Good to Great* by Jim Collins. It's an incredibly easy read that analyses why some organisations become great while others stay at good. It also put research findings behind everything I already believed as a leader.

Collins argues good is the enemy of great (or outstanding if you prefer) because it allows us to stop improving, it's good enough: 'if it ain't broke we don't need to fix it'.

There is little, if any, pain or discomfort in the world of 'good' and humans are more likely to move away from pain than move toward pleasure. I think we'd all agree that *Requires Improvement* (RI) is a painful place to be, as is *Inadequate* and *Special Measures*, so we work hard to avoid those assessments.

Sir Michael Wilshaw was tapping into human psychology when he changed the judgement of *Satisfactory* to *Requires Improvement* because, like *Good*, *Satisfactory* implies it's okay and so we perceive little pain there.

If you're reading this book because you want to know how to create your version of outstanding then I suspect you're a bit different to most and you probably perceive some level of pain in where your school currently is. For you perhaps *Good* isn't good enough?

ACTIVITY

List some reasons your school might have for not being outstanding? Next to each point, list who you think believes these reasons.

CHAPTER SUMMARY

- *Every school can be outstanding*
- *We need to be aware of and challenge the reasons why a school is not Outstanding*
- *As leaders we need to be aware that good is the enemy of great*

BONUS MATERIAL

Outstanding Head teachers Paul, Tara and Rebecca have shared their approach with Head teachers at *Heads Up* conferences. Watch their presentations at *www.ukheadsup.com/outstanding-heads-best-practice*

Chapter 2

What is getting in the way of all schools becoming outstanding?

'Always bear in mind that your own resolution
to succeed is more important than any other.'
Abraham Lincoln

In this chapter:
- *There's an elephant in the room*
- *The magic ingredient that makes a school
outstanding*

Through my work with school leaders and Heads all over the UK I have noticed patterns in what is holding schools back from being exceptional and I've made two key insights:

1. School leaders are not properly trained in how to lead adults (their staff)
2. Culture is what makes a school outstanding

Let's look at both of these claims in turn.

WE NEED BETTER LEADERSHIP TRAINING

School leaders are not properly trained in how to lead adults

This is the elephant in the room.

Pretty much every school leader I have met has a similar background: they gained a qualification in teaching, then became a newly qualified teacher, developed their classroom practice and became a competent, experienced teacher (more often than not 'outstanding'). They were given more respon-sibility and progressed through the management structure. Throughout this journey they were trained, mentored and learnt on the job. There would have been specialists, experts and role models for them to turn to, behaviour support, in-class support, educational psychologists and more. It's fair to say that most school leaders, certainly the many I've met, are really good classroom practitioners, who have worked hard to hone their craft and as a result have been given greater responsibility and impact by becoming leaders.

Now let's look at the training they received to lead adults. Usually there would be some training, be it middle leader training, the *National Professional Qualification for Headship* (NPQH), and some other courses to attend. A coach or mentor is often assigned and hopefully someone at the local authority is offering a helpful and supportive hand.

Over a number of years school leaders will attend more training, this is often a blend consisting of mainly knowledge training (that is *Life Without Levels*, developing curriculum, SEN training etc.) and some leadership skills training. I've found that there doesn't seem to be much targeted training on the leadership skills needed to guide an adult team to create an extraordinary school.

There certainly hasn't been as much training to work with adults as there has been to work with children.

When writing this book I had some excellent feedback from a Head teacher. He reviewed a draft I'd prepared and was 'a bit miffed' that I was implying Heads were not well trained in leadership skills. I respect his opinion a great deal. He is an exceptional leader and I'd say he's a natural because at a young age (in leadership terms) he has been able to create an exemplary school. But I do I disagree with him on this. I realise you may have been well taught or naturally have exceptional leadership skills, as this Head has, and if you are then that is brilliant and we can all learn a lot from you. But I'd like to explain why I have this view and the evidence it's based on.

What makes me think Heads are not properly trained in leadership skills?

I see this in the schools I work with

When I work with leadership teams on how to create a vision, how to have a successful difficult conversation or how to properly coach someone I am constantly asked, **'Why has no-one ever told me this before?'**

They didn't know this knowledge was out there and how useful it would be to them. They can apply it immediately to their team, which allows them to understand what is happening in their school and make improvements.

As one deputy said to me, **'I've never thought about changing my leadership style with adults, and yet I do this so easily with children.** That's because she is so well trained and experienced in teaching and leading children.

A London Head I worked with had two feuding Deputy Heads and reached the point where she didn't know what to do with them so she put them into an office in the hope they would fight it out and be done with it!

After working with me over the course of just two terms these deputies not only had an effective working relationship but had also forged a personal relationship so strong they would ask each other for parenting advice! The Head teacher thinks I'm a miracle worker but the fact is these deputies were willing to be mediated and coached. They were also willing to learn some skills and apply them so that they no longer needed me (or anyone) to keep their relationship working amiably.

I train Heads in leadership skills and they all recommend the training

One of the areas I've trained hundreds of Heads and school leaders on is how to have successful difficult conversations which, I'm sure you'll agree, is pretty much a daily part of life as a leader.

The fact I'm sought out for this training, it's recommended by everyone who attends and it has such an impact on achieving success with difficult conversations tells me our school leaders are not trained well-enough in this skill despite the ever growing need to tackle these troublesome conversations. One Head, who was just a few years away from retiring, said it was the best training she'd ever had and wished she'd learnt it earlier in her career. I find this disappointing because it seems we are not supporting our Heads with the skills needed for effective leadership and better schools.

When leadership is not great the whole school suffers

Conversely I have worked in schools with really fantastic teachers but with poor leadership and it is heart breaking to see the impact this can have on the team:

- Low morale
- Wasted time
- Bureaucracy over the smallest things
- Lots of unnecessary email communication
- Politics and factions within the school
- High sickness
- High staff turnover
- Late performance management

All of the above issues existed in one school I worked with. The situation was the result of poor leadership skills in the Head teacher, but I don't blame the Head, because they had not been taught the skills.

And their Governor line managers had not managed their performance well enough to notice their limitations and make them aware of them. It's true for all of us that *we don't know what we don't know.* You would hope leaders have self-awareness but we all have blind spots. When the inspectors called the school it was unsurprisingly judged as *Requires Improvement.*

Lack of leadership skills undermines the functioning of a school. And it almost doesn't matter how good everything else is, the chances are a school will struggle under poor leadership.

THE TRADITIONAL ROUTE TO LEADERSHIP DOES NOT GROW GREAT LEADERS

In the corporate world and public sectors people move into leadership positions in often the same way, through a kind of *organic* process: You're good at a job you do, enthusiastic, competent and keen to learn more so someone promotes you. You bring the same enthusiasm, competence and keenness to this job and learn the new aspects of your role and impress those around you, so much so that they promote you again. This time you have responsibility for a team and you need to lead them. The problem is you are really good at your job, but you've never been told how to lead a team. Your new role might go well, but it might not.

I've heard so many leaders from all sorts of industries say it's not their fault their team isn't performing and I can understand why they feel that way.

However if they had been trained in leadership skills they would know that their team's performance was their responsibility and they'd be taking action to correct this. Because **being good at your job does not mean you will be a good leader; it requires a combination of expertise and leadership skills.**

Sir Richard Branson is a good example of this because he has gone from record shops to developing commercial flights into space with a lot in-between. Apparently, when Sir Richard told his board he wanted to run a train company they all thought he was mad and yet we know that's exactly what he did and he didn't stop there. I understand Sir Richard's expertise is a customer-centric approach to business building, which combined with his skills as a leader make him successful in many diverse business contexts. I think an equivalent 'hallmark' of a great leader in education is an outstanding Head teacher who can move to a new school and set about making it outstanding. The new school is the new context, but the knowledge of schools (their expertise) and leadership skills are what the Head brings with them and continues to develop.

How should we develop leaders?

Many businesses and public sectors now have fast track leadership programmes which recruit people specifically to learn how to lead: the civil service, NHS, Unilever, BP, John Lewis, IBM, local councils and Head teacher fast track, to name a few, are all aimed at creating their future leaders quickly. They blend experience and leadership training and most importantly they know the training doesn't end when the scheme does. I'm not saying fast track schemes are the only way to develop leaders, but they give the important blend of experience and training and fast track schemes tend to do this better than most organically appointed leadership routes ('You're really good at your job, here, have a team to lead!'). They succeed because they have the extra element of training leadership skills. Of course a method where someone who is experienced, organically promoted and trained to lead would work just as well.

The ongoing development and support of leaders is just as important as the initial training. Let's think about a high performing athlete; imagine if Andy Murray, after winning Wimbledon in 2013, had received no more support, coaching or training. It just wouldn't happen!

Even if he kept up his physical fitness it wouldn't be enough for him to stay at the top of his game. He needs better coaches, better techniques and better trainers to continue to compete at this level.

This is the difference between good and great: Andy Murray is a great tennis player, he didn't stop at being good, he kept working until he was great and now he has to keep working hard to remain great and push towards greater. (And his 2014 dip in form after parting from Ivan Lendl shows how hard it is to maintain top level performance).

Andy Murray really focuses on his own continued professional development, which is a necessity in the world of sport.

And I think it's a necessity for anyone who wants to develop their skills and expertise in their profession.

Let's use an example closer to home, that of a good classroom teacher. They could stay at being *good,* which is good enough, however to become brilliant they will need some help and support, maybe training, shadowing, coaching, but certainly some guidance.

Leaders need the same ongoing development. **I coach a lot of Heads and one says to me at the end of every coaching conversation, 'If only everyday could start with a call to you, you make everything so much clearer for me'.** Coaching is one form of ongoing support and leadership development.

ACTIVITY

Like Andy Murray when he's strategising about the support he needs to win Wimbledon, what training and support would you need to develop even further professionally and lead at a level where you could create the school you've always wanted?

Write down what leadership books have you bought and read in the last year?

THERE IS A MAGIC INGREDIENT
WHICH MAKES A SCHOOL OUTSTANDING

The second insight I have found is that there is a magic ingredient which makes a school exceptional. You see getting to *good* is essentially a checklist, it's a hard tick list, but a tick list nonetheless of things that need to be happening regularly. **But there is a bit of magic when it comes to outstanding and that magic is all about creating the right school culture.** And culture is harder to create because it's about consistent behaviour over a stretch of time.

The difference between a *good* and *outstanding* school is like the difference between a *good* and *outstanding* lesson

Think of a consistently *good* teacher and what a lesson looks like with them. Now think of an outstanding teacher and what a lesson looks like with them.

The *good* lesson has key components and follows a checklist but when we see one of those extraordinary lessons the teacher has probably 'loosened up' from that structure to create an inspired lesson. I often hear Heads talk about how in *good* lessons the teacher will be doing the majority of the work but in the best lessons it's the children who are fully engaged.

There is a qualitative difference between a *good* and *outstanding* lesson and the same is also true at a school level.

Good schools will have good systems and processes in place which are adhered to.

Excellent schools will have these as well. However it is the culture which will be different and people will have a freedom within that structure to do things differently, take risks and excel.

Whenever I hear an outstanding Head teacher share their best practice they almost always start with their school ethos or values, essentially the culture they have created. This is the foundation for the excellence they have been able to create.

You can feel when a school is outstanding

The funny thing about a school being so brilliant is you can feel it pretty quickly. I can usually guess the Ofsted rating within a few minutes of walking in the door.

One of the best examples was a school in south London. The environment, while as good as it could have been, was anything but inviting. The reception area was tatty and tired and the school looked like it was falling apart. Yet the school felt culturally vibrant because of the staff and the wonderful way they interacted with everyone; they were like rays of sunlight. When I met the Head it turned out they were, thankfully, getting a new school building and had just been judged as *Outstanding* by Ofsted.

When a school gets stuck at 'good'...

As a Head reading this we both know you have immense pressure on you and I think you will know what I'm about to say. When a school gets stuck at *good* it's because of the Head. I know that will probably feel like a heavy burden but I think we both know it's true.

One Head I met, who was just about to retire, said being a Head was much like being a football manager: if you don't come home with that piece of *silverware* you're out on your ear!

So let's go on to look at how as a leader you can create that magic ingredient of an outstanding culture.

CHAPTER SUMMARY

- *To create the best school both school expertise and leadership skills are needed*
- *We don't always give leaders the skills they need to create high performing teams*
- *Culture is the magic ingredient which makes a school outstanding in the fullest sense.*

Chapter 3
The three core leadership strategies for creating an outstanding school culture

'It is only through consistency over time, through multiple generations, that you get maximum results.'
Jim Collins, Good to Great

In this chapter:
- *The three core leadership strategies that create a culture of excellence*
- *Culture by design instead of by accident*
- *Being in the right place to create your outstanding culture*
- *You've already created a great culture many times*
- *Working with children and adults is the same, but different*

When you became a Head you had a vision of a school which you wanted to create and the chances are you still have that school in your mind, but you have you created it yet? This requires three leadership strategies delivered well and consistently over a period of time.

You might find you are familiar with the ideas or that you are competent at using these leadership strategies. As you know I believe a lot of school leaders (and leaders in other sectors) are not well trained in the leadership skills needed to create an exceptional culture. While many are aware of these key strategies, they openly admit they have not always been trained or supported sufficiently in how to use these skills effectively.

THE THREE CORE LEADERSHIP STRATEGIES THAT CREATE AN OUTSTANDING CULTURE

1. Get everyone on board: Create a really compelling, values-based vision

2. Ensure behaviour and performance are consistently high: Have successful difficult conversations

3. Create the best people: Grow your team's strengths so they are brilliant in their role

The first strategy is to excite and motivate the team toward a shared purpose and this is done by creating a compelling vision, not just a motto like 'love, live, learn' but a clear picture of success.

The second strategy is to make sure everyone is performing and behaving to expectations, which requires having those difficult conversations successfully.

Often school leaders are more willing to talk about performance than behaviour. In fact when I mention behaviour in schools, because the focus is rightly on children, I find Heads often tell me what Ofsted rating they got for behaviour.

When I say I'm talking about adult behaviour and not children it usually gets a giggle!

The third strategy is to develop your team so they can deliver their best every day and enjoy a standard of excellence. We do this by growing their skills in a meaningful way. This is about developing the areas they need to improve and their team's strengths. Building on strengths is something that can tend to be overlooked.

GET YOUR 'SCHOOL BUS' RIGHT

I like to use the analogy created by Jim Collins of getting everyone on your *school bus*. With your vision you're telling everyone very clearly where your school is going so they can decide whether this is the bus for them or not. After all we want people on the bus who want to be there, don't we?

Once on the bus we need to make sure everyone performs and behaves well, this is where our skill in having successful difficult conversations comes in. We don't want people with their bum on the bus but their head out the window!

Then finally, with everyone wanting to be on the bus, behaving in a way that makes this a great bus to be on, we want to make sure everyone is able to give their best to this journey so we can get to our destination (our vision) sooner. So now we focus on growing the skills of our team to encourage them to be fulfilled and excel at what they do. Now we're all singing on the bus!

Implementing these three strategies means that you will be cheerfully driving your impressive school bus!

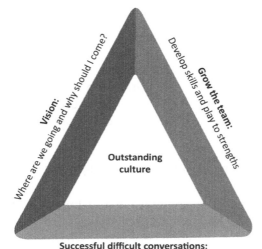

Successful difficult conversations:
Tackle performance and behaviour issues quickly and well

Figure 1: The three key leadership strategies
that create an outstanding culture

As you know a triangle is the strongest shape unless you remove any one side. In the same way if you miss any one of these core leadership strategies your culture will be pretty good but it will struggle to be truly outstanding.

ALL SCHOOLS USE THESE STRATEGIES

I'm sure you are using these three strategies. All schools I've worked with have a vision, have difficult conversations and develop their team. But what Heads tell me is:

- No-one knows our vision or what it means
- Adults are not all performing or behaving as

expected, even after a request for change
- Our staff members are being developed but they're not all yet pushing through to the level of *Outstanding*.

At core they are trying to create an exceptional level of education for their children but not attaining it. The difference in great schools is they use these proven strategies to create a superb culture.

CULTURE BY DESIGN INSTEAD OF ACCIDENT

In creating a superb school culture we are creating a culture by design. Culture happens as soon as you have two or more people come together. It's the established behavioural and social norms that a group operates within. Think about your school; it has a culture and it has pockets of culture. For example you might have a year group that you think is superb because they deliver exceptional education every day, they work well as a team, they are positive and have a can-do attitude. Conversely you might have another year group that lacks energy, doesn't want to go the extra mile and is, well, a bit of a grey cloud.

The culture equation

Culture is behaviour over time: behaviour repeated over time which becomes established and becomes the norm. When this just happens, because people have come together regularly, we have a culture which has formed by accident: it might be really good, really bad or anything in between. If we're lucky we'll have a happy accident … if we're lucky.

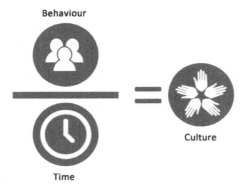

Figure 2: Our behaviour over time creates culture

However when we aim to create an outstanding culture we are creating culture by design which is achieved through those three core leadership strategies.

Creating a culture of excellence will take a few years, at least two if you go about it with determination. We are developing skills and behaviours and they take time to cultivate. While it's not for the faint-hearted it is an exciting and rewarding journey.

There are several essential factors needed to embark on creating the very best school culture.

ARE YOU IN THE RIGHT PLACE TO CREATE YOUR OUTSTANDING CULTURE?

Ofsted category

I believe this is not a journey a school judged as *Inadequate* should start while they are in that category. This is because the school is seriously failing and needs to fix this as soon as possible. The leadership style is likely to be autocratic with the team being told what to do to improve. A school needs to keep its head above water before it can really begin to look at culture. Some schools judged as *Requires Improvement* are in a ideal position to start this journey and certainly schools who are *good* should if they really aspire to excellence.

Culture is a never ending cycle of improvement and so outstanding schools can also benefit from developing their culture further.

Schools rated *Requires Improvement*

Some schools judged as *Requires Improvement* can start this journey and **the main difference I find in RI schools who are ready and schools who are not is the Head teacher**. In schools ready to develop their culture and start creating the very best culture, before they get to *good*, the Head is already looking for their school to be a centre of excellence; for them good is not good enough. At the same time they know this requires the team to take the school there and they are willing to put in the additional work required while at RI status.

In a *Requires Improvement* school, which is not yet ready to start this cultural journey, the Head is usually pretty weighed down and focused on getting to *Good*, which is no bad goal. When they get there they will be in a position to think about either consolidating at *Good* or moving to *Outstanding*.

Neither is bad, but I think it's useful to be aware of these two scenarios.

Time and energy

I know being a Head teacher is a demanding and frantically busy role and so if you are to aspire to creating an outstanding culture you will have to stretch yourself and devote time and energy to making it happen. We all have the same amount of hours in the day, and with those hours some Heads make their school *Outstanding* while others don't. I don't say this to criticise, I realise getting to *Good* is hard enough.

I say this because **I want us all to spend the one most precious resource we have, time, as wisely as possible**.

Your time must be allocated carefully in order to create the very best school you can, the one you dreamt of creating when you became a Head and one that is much, much more than Ofsted's *Outstanding*. But I have to be honest and tell you it will take considerable time and energy.

Willingness to develop

As a Head teacher you must be willing to develop your skills. Most likely your focus will be on developing your leadership skills so that you can create the best culture by design. This will mean letting go of some old habits and ways of working and adopting new ones. The same is true for your senior leadership team, but it starts with you.

YOU'VE ALREADY CREATED A GREAT CULTURE MANY TIMES

The first great team you created was your class

The exciting news is you've already been a master of creating an exceptional culture. Like me you were once a teacher, responsible for around 30 children, and in that role I bet you were fantastic. I bet your children loved you, I bet they learnt a lot with you and I bet you are one of the teachers they warmly remember. You created a dazzling team with that class, a team that performed well, was flexible when things changed (and don't they always in school!), behaved beautifully and grew as individuals as well as a cohesive group.

You excelled at classroom management, be it lining up and going into assembly (and your class was probably noticed for this), or having lively and interactive lessons which could have descended into chaos but, because of how you scaffolded activities, were actually wonderfully memorable learning experiences; the kind children are excited to talk about when they get home.

As a brilliant class teacher you wouldn't have accepted any excuse for your class not progressing well, in fact they probably made rapid progress with you.

Watch out for those excuses

As a Head you will probably have heard teachers or TAs talk about why a class isn't progressing enough and if they are saying things like 'it's the demographic' I imagine you wouldn't accept this as a valid reason. The same is true at a whole school level and you've got to be really aware of these excuses, in disguise as reasons, and not let them be the reason you or your team believe you can't be *Outstanding*. Be alert to excuses like those covered earlier which can seduce us into believing it's not possible to be *Outstanding*:

> *'It's the demographic of this school'*

> *'It's the staff we have in this school,*
> *they don't perform well enough'*

> *'We don't have enough money, resources,*
> *teachers, TAs.'*

I hear dedicated Heads, who I'm sure can make their school outstanding, talk about their demographic as being the reason they can't improve. However other schools have overcome these issues and if they can do it the rest of us can too.

I believe that being a teacher really helped me achieve success in business because **there are so many skills you have as a teacher that are so important when leading adults.**

Let's look at what you did as a class teacher that created a fantastic team of children, in fact an outstanding culture, year after year.

You talked about your vision daily

Even though you probably didn't have an explicit vision for your class you would have referred to it on a regular basis in a range of ways. You might have talked about how 'we're a class who always tries our best', how 'we always set our work out neatly'; in lots of little ways you would have told your class what your picture of success was for them.

You set out expectations of behaviour and stuck to them

Think about September, faced with a new class, you quickly set about establishing your class rules. Chances are they were the same as elsewhere in the school, you'd think that your pupils would know them by now so you didn't need to reinforce them; but you do. This is the first part of establishing what the behaviour of your class (your team) will be.

You sanctioned appropriately

Having set out your expectations, when they were not met you sanctioned appropriately. You would have focused more on behaviour than the child: 'Jack, because you are talking during silent reading I am going to give you a first warning which I hope you can earn back', instead of 'Jack you are naughty boy, stop talking'.

You praised

You would have praised your children, their tables and the class for getting things right, reinforcing their good behaviour. And you would have praised more than you sanctioned. You would have looked for those children who didn't often 'get it right', who were often in trouble for their behaviour and found ways to praise them, to encourage them, to give them some responsibility so they could shine and you could acknowledge them. But you also made sure you did this with the quieter ones, no child was left unnoticed for praise in your class. And you would have been specific in your praise for their work and their behaviour 'Jack is sitting so nicely, with his arms folded and looking at the board, well done Jack', again reinforcing and sharing your vision and expectations.

You were relentless in developing your children's skills

These questions would have been a big focus: Were your lessons achieving the outcome? Were they developing knowledge and skills? What did you need to do to help pupils who were struggling? Developing your children would have been central to all you did.

You created useful structures to support the class

Be it silent reading every morning for 15 minutes, monitor jobs for children, reward systems or even the order the class would line up in, you created structures to help order the day and let your class know what was coming next, as far as any class teacher can (and let's face it, we've all faced the unexpected experience when our class is ready for indoor PE only to find out we can't use the hall!). You put in place whatever you needed to help you manage your class and let them have a stimulating learning culture every day.

Each of these elements are part of the three core strategies:

Vision	You talked about your vision daily
	You praised
Difficult conversations	You set out expectations of behaviour and stuck to them
	You sanctioned appropriately
Growth	You were relentless in developing your children's skills
	You created useful structures to support the class

And as a result you created a great team and culture. Your class would have taken on an identity of its own, a team spirit which grew throughout the year. Class assemblies and school competitions would have given your class a chance to shine, but smaller wins throughout every day and week will have helped as well.

Over time you saw your class grow into a unit, a team, achieving whole group success as well as individual success.

Think about a class in September and that same class in July, they're different aren't they? And different in a good way, more relaxed, more of a team, more capable and more fun to be with. You created that great team, that culture, as teacher so why is it harder to do with adults?

WORKING WITH CHILDREN IS THE SAME AS WORKING WITH ADULTS, BUT DIFFERENT!

There are many parallels with how we work with children that apply to adults. In fact there is almost always an equivalent scenario because they are essentially the same in principle. But working with children and working with adults is different in subtlety.

I was working with a wonderful group of Heads in the north and one Head was telling us how a teacher in her school had told off her whole class because two children had misbehaved.

Unsurprisingly some of the children were upset and their parents complained to the school.

I'm sure you will agree, as did I and the other Heads, that the teacher should have spoken to the two children and not told off the whole class. I asked the Heads if they'd ever had a staff meeting where they had raised an issue like checking emails, or being in school on time, or getting the class to assembly promptly. 'Oh yes' they nodded smiling.

And so I asked if when they gave that message if there were a few people in particular they knew the message was for, a few people who didn't check their email regularly, who were late into school or in getting their class into assembly. 'Oh yes' they nodded. So I asked them how is that different from telling off a whole class for two children's behaviour?

They gasped and then laughed, a light bulb moment: they could see it clearly now, but never had before.

It's funny but what we do so naturally and obviously with children doesn't always easily translate across to working with adults. Creating a great adult team feels harder than working with a class of children, at least that seems to be the case in education (outside of education a lot of people seem to find it hard to create great adult teams and are scared of working with children!). I often have Heads email me to say they'd pick working with children over adults any day! From what I have observed through my work in schools I think this is the case for three reasons.

Three reasons it seems adults are harder to work with than children

Adults don't need to be told

There seems to be an implicit belief that by time we are adults we almost don't need to be told, that we can figure a lot of things out by ourselves. To an extent this is true but it's not enough for us to rely on.

We don't see our own behaviour but everyone else does and we don't always realise the impact we have on others, positive or negative, so we can't rely on knowing all of this ourselves; we sometimes need others to help us, to tell us.

Peer to peer relationships

Adult communication is hard because you are dealing with peers. Even in a hierarchy, these are other adults regardless of their position and so they are peers.

The very nature of being a class teacher, an adult with a class of children, means we have a position of greater knowledge, experience and authority. With adults we might be dealing with people who are older than us, who have been in their role longer, who have been in our school longer, who believe they know more than us, who we believe know more than us! And all of this can make it harder to go about creating a great team. **Peer to peer relationships in a hierarchical structure just feel harder.**

It was once the same when we worked with children, which I'm sure you can recall. I remember when I was training to be a teacher, my heart would race and I would think 'How am I going to get a class of children to listen, behave and learn with me?'. It doesn't cross my mind now because I have been trained in the skills I need and I'm experienced at using them.

We don't have all the skills

In leadership roles, even if you have been a great class teacher there are additional skills and knowledge which make it easier to lead adults well. I've touched on this already but think about how well trained you have been to be a teacher and how much experience you have.

Have you had a comparable level of training for leading adults as you have for children? Sadly the answer I'm often told by school leaders is 'no'.

ACTIVITY

Thinking about your school bus write down:
Who really gets your vision? Who doesn't? Who
performs to the level you want them to? Who doesn't?
Whose skills are constantly developing and improving?
Whose are not? You might like to think of a group like your
leadership team or teachers.

CHAPTER SUMMARY

- *Culture is a crucial foundation for creating an outstanding school*
- *Creating a high performing culture requires three leadership strategies:*

  1. Vision: Tell people where you want to go
  2. Ensure behaviour and performance are consistently high: Have successful difficult conversations
  3. Create the best people: Grow your team's strengths so they are brilliant in their role

- *Culture takes years to develop*

- *The core skills are the same when working with children and adults. Remember: You've already created a great team as a class teacher.*
- *Working with adults can feel harder for three reasons:*

  1. We can often think adults don't need to be told
  2. We don't have the same authority we have in class, in fact we have much harder peer to peer relationships in a hierarchical structure
  3. We don't have all the skills we need to create our great adult team

Chapter 4
It's all down to leadership

'Leaders aren't born, they are made. And they are made just like anything else, through hard work. And that's the price we'll have to pay to achieve our goal, or any goal.'
Vince Lombardi

In this chapter:
- *It's all down to leadership*
- *Great leaders have the best teams*
- *Becoming a greater leader*

As Head teacher you are the leader of your school and the leader of the next generation; you know too well that your school's success ultimately rests on your shoulders. So before we get onto how you can start creating a vibrant culture by creating your vision, having more successful difficult conversations and developing your team (the 'exciting part') it's important to touch on a few points about leadership because leadership is what makes all of this work.

Leadership creates culture by design; a lack of leadership allows a culture to form by accident.

ACTIVITY

Work out approximately how many children will pass through your school while you are leader. In about 30 years they will be running the country.

LEADERSHIP IS THE SHEPHERD
OF HIGH PERFORMANCE

Leadership enables all of this; by mastering the three leadership strategies you can create a high performance culture, your dream school. Your job is to lead your team to success, to shepherd them and show them the way.

GREAT LEADERS CREATE GREAT CULTURES

The behaviour of individuals, consistently repeated over time, creates a culture. Great leaders know this and keep using the three key strategies to create the right culture for their school. The classroom, again, provides a fantastic example of this at work, so let's look specifically at classroom behaviour, which is the class-based counterpart to the strategy of having successful difficult conversations.

When a teacher creates a good classroom environment they will foster co-operative class behaviour and systems of reward and sanction to ensure these remain in place.

Some teachers will tirelessly reinforce the behaviour they expect until it becomes normal and as a result they will create a good classroom culture with clear expectations of pupil behaviour that allows them to get on with the job of teaching and learning.

Other teachers will be more inconsistent, sometimes reinforcing the behaviour they expect, sometimes using sanctions and sometimes not. There will be a culture in this classroom but not the best culture possible because of this inconsistency of the leader (in this case the teacher) in enforcing what is and isn't okay. They will continue to have behaviour issues that will distract from the job of teaching and learning.

It is the consistent implementation of the strategy that makes it work.

GREAT LEADERS CREATE THE BEST TEAMS

Leadership teams

Any leader who complains that their leadership team is not good enough sadly only has themselves to blame (unless they have just taken on the role). Great leaders take responsibility and so if your leadership team isn't performing well enough then you have to fix it, the reason this is often hard is because we don't train Heads on how to do this.

When I worked in retail I asked a senior leader who the best shop floor manager was in their branch. They answered quickly, enthusiastically telling me about why a certain manager was so good. I then asked what this shop floor manager's section managers were like, how good were they? Apparently they were terrible! So how could the shop floor manager be so good if their team wasn't?

It turns out the shop floor manager was doing all the things their section managers should have been doing which made him look wonderfully busy and motivated, which he was, but on all the wrong things.

ACTIVITY

I want you to daydream for a little while about what your leadership team would look like if they were performing at the level you wanted them to?

- *What would meetings look like?*
- *How would it feel to be part of this team?*
- *What would you say about the team?*
- *What would team members be doing?*
- *How would the rest of your school feel about your team?*

After your day dream jot down some notes, or draw a picture if you prefer, to capture what you saw.

Great leaders grow their leader's skills

Leadership is a skill, in fact it's a set of skills, and great leaders cultivate leadership skills in their leaders. They develop management knowledge and skills, like budgeting and strategic planning, but also core leadership skills that centre around leading and managing people such as having difficult conversations well and growing their best. **If you're going to create your amazing school your leadership team needs to help you most.**

Heads often ask me to teach their leadership teams how to have successful difficult conversations for two reasons. Firstly they know this is a skill and skills need practice so the sooner their senior leaders learn the skill the sooner they can start practising and become good at it. A lot of Heads tell me they were never trained in having difficult conversations, and those who have learnt the skill have often done so because they needed to have a lot of difficult conversations (usually because their school was judged RI or worse). They learnt the hard way through trial and error. The second reason for training their leaders is so issues can be dealt with closer to where they arise and not passed up to the Head to sort out. This is a more effective way of dealing with issues and frees up some of your time.

Great leaders make themselves redundant

A great leadership team should be able to run the show without you because great leaders make the need for their input redundant. If this feels a bit scary, don't worry, that's natural, but please understand that **not many people are able to lead at a level which makes their input redundant.** This level of leadership is highly valuable and therefore unlikely to lead to real redundancy, but more likely to bigger and greater roles.

To do this great leaders give more and more management and, where possible, leadership responsibility to the team so they can run the school without you; essentially everyone becomes a leader. This includes decision making responsibility so that you are not needed for every decision and, ideally, for a decreasing number of decisions. It not only means the school runs smoothly without you being there but it also prepares those leaders for future leadership roles all within the safe environment of your stewardship. Maybe you had a Head whom did that for you when you were developing as a leader?

THE LIFE CYCLE OF LEADERSHIP

Having an understanding of the leadership life-cycle, and the trap within it, is useful to leaders as it helps them understand where they have been, where they are now and where they want to go to next. It looks like this:

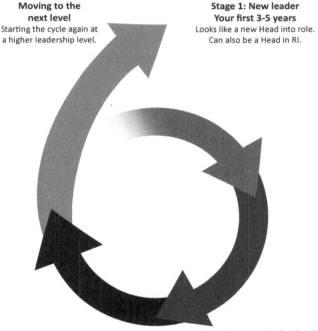

Moving to the next level
Starting the cycle again at a higher leadership level.

**Stage 1: New leader
Your first 3-5 years**
Looks like a new Head into role.
Can also be a Head in RI.

**Stage 3: Leaders of leaders
10+ years**
A respected and effective leader.
Looks like an Outstanding Head teacher.

**Stage 2: Maturing leadership
3-10 years**
An experienced Head.
Can be a Head in RI or Good who is moving to Outstanding.

Figure 3: The leadership life cycle

Some people will go all the way through the life cycle, some will stop at certain stages and some will get stuck and want to know how to move to the next stage. Whilst I have indicated how long is spent in each stage these are not absolute, they are general patterns I've noticed and the time in each stage will vary from person to person.

Stage 1: New leader – your first 3 – 5 years

Here you are learning the role. You learn the functional management aspects of the role, such as the performance management cycle, child protection, Governors meetings etc. You also learn leadership concepts (like why a vision is important) and you start developing your leadership skills. There are lots of learning mistakes made.

Examples:
- A new Head into role
- A Head in RI.

Stage 2: Maturing leadership - 3 – 10 years

Now you are learning to be a leader. You understand your role and are competent in many, if not all, the functional aspects. Now you learn and hone your leadership skills, such as inspiring a team and leading them to greater success.

Examples:
- An experienced Head
- An *RI* or *Good* Head moving to *Outstanding*.

Stage 3: Leader of leaders - 10+ years

Now you lead other leaders, in fact you are a leader's leader: a role model and inspiration to leaders. You are competent in management however you spend your time leading, not on management tasks. Other staff members carry out most, if not all, management activities. You know how to create a team that achieves excellence in all they do. You are now ready to use your skills more widely, such as supporting or leading other schools.

Examples:
- A respected leader who others look to.
- An *Outstanding* Head teacher.

Working through the life cycle

The speed you progress through the lifecycle varies from person to person. Someone on the *Head teacher Fast-track Scheme* might get to Stage 2 more quickly because of the training they've had, as might someone who doesn't take a career break to start a family, as might someone who is naturally a leader.

I once coached a deputy head who was clearly a natural leader, without being a Head she was already demonstrating the characteristics of a mature leader and could easily have gone on to be a leader of leaders. I still watch her career unfold with great interest.

But please don't think speed is the be all and end all. Quality of leadership is far more important and I refer to speed simply because people will progress through these stages at different paces. Whilst people progress at difference speeds I have found that there tends to be a point where a leader can get stuck.

Getting stuck at Stage 2

Most Heads will progress to Stage 2 between three to ten years into their career. At this stage they know how to do the job well but are not yet the great leaders they could be because they haven't developed their leadership skills fully. And this is where a leader can get stuck. This is because in Stage 2 you can be a competent Head and as we know good is the enemy of great.

You could say competency is good's ally because at Stage 2 you are competent in your role, which means you are in your comfort zone and good at what you do.

Moving to Stage 3 means you will have to move out of your comfort zone and the motivator to do this is usually one of 'towards pleasure', which as I have already discussed is generally not as motivating as moving away from pain. In the process of moving out of your comfort zone you create pain because stretching comfort zones is usually a bit, well, uncomfortable. Moving to different schools, taking on challenges like amalgamating schools and having a new school built will all develop a leader, and these challenges may or may not develop the leadership skills they need to take their leadership to that of Stage 3, an extraordinary Head who is regarded as a leader of leaders.

I hope you can see how Stage 2 is place where a leader can remain. It's not a bad place for a leader to stay but it doesn't lead to great. It's like the student whom is happy achieving a grade C, but for their own reasons does not strive to achieve an A.

My question to you is: What grade from A* to C do you want for your school?

The dual role of Heads as managers and leaders

In the life cycle of leadership you will see there is a transition from being a manager to being a leader. Neither is better than the other. Both are needed to lead well: if a leader isn't able to make sure their school is being well managed it doesn't matter how capable they are at leading because their school operation won't function well.

In some organisations this isn't as huge a challenge as it is in schools because there are teams who take care of the operation, freeing up the leader to focus on leadership.

You and I know that in schools, particularly primary schools, managing and leading falls mainly to the Head and senior leadership team and so you need to be able to manage through others so you can become a 'leader of leaders'.

Figure 4 illustrates how the amount of managing and leading changes over the course of the leadership life cycle.

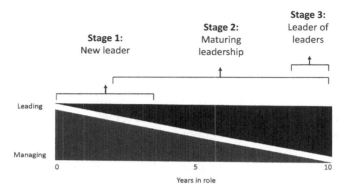

Figure 4: Illustration of the amount of management and leadership required at different stages of the leadership life cycle.

Stage 1: New leader – your first 3 – 5 years

Management	Become good at the management activities e.g. budgeting, child protection, policy implementation, School Improvement Plan.
Leadership	Learn about leadership, your own leadership style and start developing these skills but management is your priority.

Stage 2: Maturing leadership - 3 – 10 years

Management	Increasingly train and delegate activities and responsibilities to leadership team. Start to reduce the time you spend on management.
Leadership	Start to develop and increase your leadership skills.

Stage 3: Leader of leaders - 10+ years

Management	Low level monitoring – the school can now run without you.
Leadership	Create a high performing team with exceptional results (in the fullest sense, not just tests) and support other leaders in other schools.

CREATING THE SCHOOL YOU HAVE ALWAYS WANTED TO LEAD

The rest of this book is dedicated to helping you develop your skills in the three core leadership strategies. You might have some already or you might want to improve on others. Wherever you are I believe, and hope, you will benefit from reading on.

These are skills though and skills require practice in the same way as if you were learning to play the guitar: I could show you how to play a C chord, I could ask you to have a go at playing a C chord and after a perhaps a few goes you could do this well, but if you don't pick up that guitar for a week the chances are you won't be able to play a C chord. Skills require practice and you are probably aware of various models of learning, including the learning hierarchy:

Acquire
You are learning the skill but don't use it fluently. The aim here is be accurate in using it so that the skill is truly acquired.

Fluency
You can complete the task accurately but not quickly so the aim here is to increase speed whilst maintaining accuracy.

Generalisation
You are now fluent and accurate in the skill but do not use it in other situations; the aim now is to generalise the skill to wider settings.

Adaptation
You now generalise the skill but do not adapt the skills to new setting. The aim now is to adapt the skill or it's component parts to new situations.

Figure 5: Learning Hierarchy
Haring, Lovitt, Eaton, & Hansen, 1978

Learning or developing skills often takes us out of our comfort zone. If we want something enough then we are usually willing to stretch, so the question is: **Are you willing to stretch yourself in order to create the best education you can for your school children?**

If your answer is a yes then your comfort zone is ready to be stretched and the good news is once you've expanded your comfort zone it doesn't shrink back, you automatically have a larger comfort zone for keeps!

I wouldn't be surprised if you feel like it's a lot to do; it is, but I hope what I will make it easier. Over the rest of this book I'd like to share with you the work I do with schools to help them make a culture of excellence through these three strategies.

I've shared this information with hundreds of school leaders up and down the UK and I'm proud to say they have loved and learnt from it. Most importantly I hope you enjoy it and find it useful.

CHAPTER SUMMARY

- *Leaders create culture through their teams*
- *Know where you are on the leadership life cycle*
- *Be aware of getting stuck in Stage 2, unless it is a conscious choice*

Section 2
The three core leadership strategies that make an outstanding school culture

Chapter 5

Tell them where you are going and why

*'Efforts and courage are not enough
without purpose and direction.'*
John F. Kennedy

If, as a leader, no-one is following you you're just going for a walk! Having a clear vision let's other decide if they want to follow you.

In this chapter:
- *Why vision is so important*
- *A vision should be like Marmite*
- *How life gets easier with a vision*
- *How a good vision works with our brain
  to motivate others*
- *A step by step process to creating your vision*

THINGS GET EASIER
WHEN YOU HAVE A CLEAR VISION

Better decisions and actions

A clear vision gives direction to the team and as such it guides decisions. It stops you being pulled off track from what you want to create in your school.

Let's face it, there is so much bombarding you in school it's easy to get pulled off track. There is so much you could do it can be confusing to know what to take on. A vision helps you decide.

People can vote with their feet

A clear vision let's people decide if they want to join you on this journey and as a leader you need to enable your team to make this choice. The first and most important step is to know your vision and communicate it clearly.

Easy to remember

A clear vision is easy to remember. Catchy, snappy mottos are usually good because they are easy to remember but they often don't go far enough in articulating a clear direction. Our brains are designed to remember pictures, images and emotions and we need to use this information when creating our vision.

I worked with a wonderful school to help them develop their vision: they had invested a lot of time working on it with Governors, teachers, the leadership team and as they said to me when we started working together 'Our vision is just words, they are what we want, but they don't inspire us'. We worked on what the vision looked like through a variety of creative means which were put up all over the walls in the room we were working in; when other staff saw these the Head received many comments of 'Is this what you want for the school? Great, we can to that' and off they marched with determination.

The Head and leadership team were amazed at the impact the vision had on their team and the Head told me she'd been trying to get people to understand it for years and they hadn't until now.

GREAT LEADERS CREATE A COMPELLING VISION

Great leaders create a deeply compelling vision, one which gives clear direction and motivation to the team. This vision is more than an order or to do list and more than a motto. It resonates at a deeper level with the team and with those who come into contact with it. It provides purpose to everything they do, it guides their decisions and energises them. I've helped many schools craft their vision. They ask me to consult because they know something in their vision isn't working; it's full of nice words but not generating the momentum they want. Often they have a motto or mission but not a vision.

VISION IS A NECESSARY COURTESY OF LEADERSHIP

I believe a vision is a necessary courtesy of leadership. If I want you to follow me then really I need to tell you our destination. If I keep it a secret then would you follow me? Probably not, and if you did follow me blindly you wouldn't be able to contribute much because you would be stumbling around in the dark! I would have failed to excite you by sharing my vision.

It's a bit like going on a holiday. I say to you 'I'm going on holiday, do you want to come?' You want to know where, I say, 'Don't worry, it's going to be great, trust me on this one.' Eventually I manage to persuade you. Great! You wonder what to pack, you end up packing a bit of everything to be on the safe side, jumpers and shorts, jeans and summer tops, thick socks and sandals.

Will you enjoy it when we get there? Who knows?

Can you commit to this holiday fully? Unlikely. Can you prepare for it properly and bring things that will make it enjoyable? No.

Now if I say 'We're going skiing' what does that do? You might think 'I love skiing!' Or 'I hate skiing!' Or 'I've never been skiing before!'. You're certainly in a better position to decide if you want to go and if you do decide to ski you can get excited and have a far better idea of what to pack to make it a fun holiday.

Visions are the same in that we must tell people where we're going, even if it seems obvious, so they can decide if they want to come on the journey. But what's challenging about a vision is they are harder to get clear and articulate than most people think.

Deep down we know what we want but the skill is digging to find the buried treasure of the inspiring vision. Few leaders are trained or supported in this vital excavating skill!

To understand how to create your inspiring vision I'm going to share some gems about what makes a vision work.

WHAT MAKES A VISION WORK?

The great visionaries

I know you've heard about great visions and their importance and we have some sparkling examples.

Apple had Steve Jobs as the visionary to create technology that didn't require a huge manual to understand but the technology that was beautiful, powerful and easy to use, a far cry from the days of opening your new VCR or DVD and having to wade through a manual in 12 different languages to find out how to get the thing set up (and you probably never attempting to figure out how to work some of those added features you bought it for because it meant deciphering the complex manual!).

What about the Wright Brothers' vision of human flight! And Henry Ford who believed cars would replace the horse! Dr Martin Luther King who championed racial equality as did Nelson Mandela.

I don't think it's a coincidence that these visionaries created radical changes in their field. There were others attempting similar feats, but these were the ones who were most successful in achieving their vision and creating a lasting legacy. You can do the same to create a powerful vision and compelling direction for your team to charge behind.

WHAT A GREAT VISION IS NOT

Firstly I want to cover what a great vision is not. A great vision is not one or more sentences with lots of adjectives and adverbs, for example:

To create a school where children are enabled, empowered and supported to be the person they want to be.

To deliver exceptional education which excites, inspires and challenges children and teachers.

Whilst we might agree with the message these don't tell us what this looks like and they are hard to remember, as many Heads say to me: they are just words. To me they are bit like personal ads:

Head teacher seeks
intelligent, child-centred, creative, enthusiastic, team player with GSOH to educate and develop the whole child, create a love of learning and the citizens of tomorrow.'

They are also *not* ten point plans:

1. Create stimulating learning environments
2. Move all teaching to at least *Good*
3. Increase the use of AFL in all year groups

And so on. You will want a practical plan to achieve your vision, but this is separate piece of work.

VISIONS MUST BE COMPELLING

Creating a vision is not a tick box exercise, it's not about just having a statement on the wall that looks nice or just fulfils the requirement of having a vision.

A vision must excite and engage your team, it must be so desirable, so compelling that your team is motivated toward the picture of success. I know I use the word compelling a lot but it is the perfect word to describe what a vision must do because comes from two Latin words:

'Com' which means 'together'
'Pellere' which means 'to drive'

So literally 'compellere' means 'to drive together' and that is exactly what a vision should do; it should mobilise and inspire your team to drive towards your vision together. A vision is like a banner for your team to march behind, boldly declaring where you are going and why.

A VISION SHOULD BE LIKE MARMITE

A vision should feel impossible. If we think about Henry Ford believing the car would replace the horse, this would have seemed ludicrous to people at the time. Cars were expensive and required maintenance and were unreliable; the idea was just crazy! It's like me saying personal jet packs will replace the car and everyone will travel through the air. Does that sound a bit outlandish? Jet packs exist but not in any great quantity and they seem to be too temperamental to have everyone strap on and risk falling out of the sky! Ford's vision would have been equally ridiculous to most people at the time and would have excited some risk takers. Even if they didn't fully understand how, the idea that everyone would drive a car and travel distances quickly would have sounded hard but worth the effort.

SHOULD THE TEAM CREATE THE VISION?

I'm often asked if a vision should be created as a whole school team or by a smaller group. To me these are two approaches.

Creating a vision as a whole team is often believed to foster committed buy-in because everyone has input. I think this can work and I have seen examples where it has, but mostly it doesn't work because a lot of compromise happens in a large group which dilutes the vision so whilst everyone might like it no-one is passionate about it.

A vision without passion is a 'vision fail'! Also taking just one day to create a vision is insufficient but often that's all the time available for whole team involvement. I find it takes quite a few days of pretty intense thinking to create a strong vision.

My personal view about creating a vision as a whole school is summed up by the phrase, **'A camel is a horse designed by a committee.'**

A Head once told me how her whole school had created their vision with the children and parents involved over several exciting days.

I listened intently because I was curious to know how they had done this so well and then, as a throwaway comment, she said 'I can't remember what the vision was now' and my heart sank. After all that wonderful work the vision hadn't stuck with the Head, of all people!

I'm not sure my view is popular but I believe that leaders create a vision not in isolation but with a group, usually the school's leadership team and sometimes middle managers (Governors have also been included at times). When they have created a vision they really believe in (not just some nice sounding words), as long as they communicate it powerfully, most people, if not all, get on board. In fact of all the schools I've worked with the vision has been embraced by very nearly all the team (I can only think of one teacher who decided not to sign up to where the school was going).

Think back to the great visionaries, they would have crafted their vision through their experience and by talking to their team and others, but ultimately they pulled it all together and, in essence, presented it back to the team. They would have then listened to feedback and used it to strengthen, not dilute, their inspiring message.

NOT EVERYONE WILL LIKE YOUR VISION AND THAT'S OK

Don't worry about whether everyone in the team will like your vision, in an ideal world they will, but in reality a vision should let people decide if they are up for the journey or not. **A vision should enable your team to make a choice about their commitment to it.** Some people would have been keen to join Henry Ford, others would have thrown him in a lunatic asylum!

This clarity about goals allows people to make a decision and the more it can polarise opinions the better because if you're aiming to achieve something great you don't want people who are sitting on the fence, or trundling along, doing it just for the pay and not being engaged. You want people who will champion the school's aspirations, talk about the vision with pride and believe in its value, and do everything they can to achieve it.

The trouble is it's pretty difficult to articulate a vision and understanding our brain, in particular the limbic system, helps explain why. We know what we want emotionally deep down in the limbic system, but this part of the brain sadly isn't good with words!

HOW A GREAT VISION WORKS WITH OUR BRAIN

The limbic system

What I love about psychology, the study of mind and behaviour, is that it researches what people do and breaks it down so knowledge can be shared and we can learn from these discoveries. In the case of creating a vision we can look at who does this well, how they do it and how we can emulate it. What fascinates me about vision is that it directly taps into theories about the brain and helps us understand what our vision needs to evoke in order to be effective.

There are many theories of the brain and no one theory explains everything perfectly because it is such an interconnected and complex organ. However there are some common themes and I like to use a version of Paul D MacLean's (MacLean, 1990) *Triune Theory of the Brain*, which helps us understand the brain in a simple way, although please note it is not perfect (and I'm not a neuroscientist!).

If you were to look at a cross section of the brain you would see roughly three circular areas.

The smallest of these is your brain stem and adjoining areas, which connects your brain to your body, and keeps everything working and has basic instinctive responses. The middle circle is your limbic system; this is where our memories, feelings, emotions, values and attitudes are stored. It's the area of the brain that is concerned with keeping you alive, well and safe. The limbic system tunes in and starts ringing alarm bells when you are in a situation that doesn't feel safe, even if logically and rationally it is. It is the emotional centre of the brain. And then we have the neo-cortex, which is where our logic, rationality and higher cognitive functions reside including the brain functions responsible for speech. If you have a maths problem to solve it's your neo-cortex that works it out.

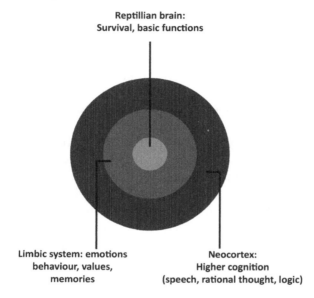

Figure 6: A summary of The Triune Brain Model

The limbic system and neocortex have been called different things by different people:

- Nobel prize winner Daniel Kahneman (Kahneman, 2011) calls them System 1 (limbic) and System 2 (neo-cortex)
- Neuroscientist MacLean calls them *your old mammal* (limbic) and *new mammal brain* (neo-cortex)
- Psychiatrist Dr Steve Peters (Peters, 2011) calls them your chimp (limbic) and your human brain (neo-cortex)

You could also say that the limbic system is the unconscious mind and the neo-cortex is the conscious mind.

To demonstrate the power of your limbic system think of a time when you've had to make a tough decision. Perhaps you spoke to people whose opinion you trust, you might have written out a list of pros and cons, you might have sought some expert advice and then when you came to make the decision you thought, 'I know option A makes sense, it's the most logical thing to do but it doesn't feel right so I'm going with option B'. Sound familiar?

Option A, the logical decision, was a neo-cortex decision and option B, the gut feeling, was a limbic system decision. Have you ever gone with the logical option A only to later say something to the effect of 'I should have listened to my gut in the first place and gone with option B'? This doesn't mean our limbic system and neo-cortex are always at odds; easy decisions are ones where they both agree, but when they do disagree, it seems that our limbic system is the one who gets it right most of the time.

Visions need to be values based

The limbic system also holds our values and this is why it's important to tell people not only where you are going but why you are going there. If a vision sets out why as well as where you're going it is easier for people to decide if this aligns with their values. If it does they will be likely to join you on your journey and make it their own, but if it doesn't then they won't be coming along!

Values speak directly to our limbic brain and when we share out vision we need to talk to other people's limbic brain; their emotional centre.

The problem with the limbic system

This all sounds nice and easy, let's get clear on our values, figure out our vision and get talking to each other's limbic system. The problem with the limbic system is that it's not articulate; it doesn't have the capacity for language which is why we often talk about 'gut decisions' and other vague explanations. If you've ever walked into a room and thought you could cut the air with a knife it's unlikely you were able to break down what led you to sense the difficult atmosphere in the room. That's your limbic system at work. It knows there's an atmosphere but struggles to fully explain why.

It is because our own vision resides in our limbic system that figuring out and telling people our vision can be half the battle; the limbic system works in emotions and pictures, not words. And when we are talking to people about our vision it's really important that we communicate to their limbic system, it's why a vision which is a list of words which make sense consciously (to our neo-cortex), doesn't appeal in the same way as something like Dr Martin Luther King's *I believe* speech which spoke to both parts of our brains.

The neo-cortex uses language and it seems to like to give us lots of descriptive words which sadly don't always inspire us in the way we want; yet we know this is possible because we've seen eloquent people inspire with the power of words. We need both brains at work and we need to help overcome the limbic system's communication challenges.

I think half the challenge is understanding your vision and half the challenge is communicating it. I'm sure you've been told many times the importance of a vision, but have you been shown how to create one that moves people? Most (and I mean very nearly all) the school leaders I have worked with haven't. My solution takes care of both understanding your vision and communication at the same time.

CREATING YOUR VISION

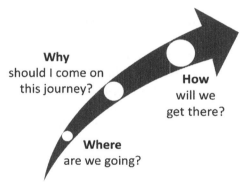

Figure 7: A good vision tells people where you are going and why, then the plan tells them how you will achieve it.

To create your compelling vision you need to tell people where you are going, why you are going there and how you will get there. This vision is best worked on as a group, usually your leadership team, so when I refer to 'you' it's this group I'm referring to.

Step 1: People need to know why

Great visions are values based; let's face it very few people truly get behind a vision that is only about becoming really rich because it's just not fulfilling. We've all heard stories of people who have earned a load of money only to jack it all in to do something more meaningful. In schools this is not such an issue because working in education is a naturally fulfilling environment because fulfilment is mostly about helping others. And so are great visions. People need to know why you want what you want: are your intentions honourable and for the good of others or self-centred personal glory? They can then understand if your vision resonates with who they are.

Define your school culture

We need to understand your core values for your school because these will define your school's culture. I find values an interesting topic because most people talk about values as being honesty, integrity, trust etc. These are values that role off the tongue but there are many more than these.

Values are what we find important; they drive our behaviour, they help us make decisions and they exist in a hierarchy. For example whilst honesty is a value for a lot of people it's not everyone's top value, this doesn't mean they are not honest it simply means that there are other values that are more important to them, such as relationships, harmony, or personal growth.

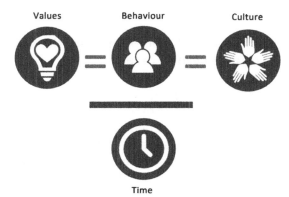

Figure 8: Our values lead to our behaviour
and our behaviour over time lead to culture.

Values drive behaviour and behaviour over time creates culture. One way you can start to understand what values are important to you as a school is to think about the behaviour you want to see in your school. If you want people to be respectful then respect is a core value, if you want people to be creative, creativity is another, if you want people to strive for the best, then excellence might be another cherished value.

ACTIVITY

Picture in your mind what you would see people doing in your perfect school, children and adults, make notes on the behaviour you see and then think about what values this shows. Pick up to five values you want to have in your school.

Don't worry if they are not fully living and breathing in the school now, these are the ones you want in the school you dream of leading.

Once you have five describe what each looks like when it is being lived by everyone in your school. What would you see? For example for the value of respect you might expect to see:

- Everyone speaking respectfully to one another.
- Respect for the environment which is always tidy, even around the coat pegs where people pick up any coats that have slipped off their peg.
- Respect for each other's time, so meetings start on time and are focused and efficient.

The list goes on, but as you can see when you start to drill into what respect would look like in your school there is a lot to consider and this is good because it helps everyone understand what we mean by respect and leads to a collective understanding. So suppose I'm late for a meeting, I will know that I'm not showing the core value of respect, which is important to the ethos of this school. This clear understanding of how we demonstrate the core value of respect allows everyone to express it more widely in behaviour. We don't want to 'legislate' for all behaviour because that's impossible; we just want to paint a clear picture of the behaviour we expect.

BRING YOUR VALUES TO LIFE

The clearer you are in what your values mean the more chance you have of achieving them. Words alone are not enough; sentences are better and stories are even better.

You can use real stories from around the school to bring your values to life; these reinforce your direction and progress. Teachers and school leaders are skilled at doing this with children, be it pointing out who is lining up nicely or telling a story after break about how one child cared for another child in the playground. These stories tell pupils what behaviour is desired and reinforce the benefits of showing such behaviour. The same needs to be done with adults.

When I was a newly qualified teacher (NQT) my classroom used to be a mess at the end of the day and I would go around picking up the pencils from the floor. I realised I needed a tidy table reward system. My class took to it enthusiastically, so I upped the ante by giving tables an area of the classroom to tidy as well, which would earn them a class point.

One day, as they quickly and carefully tidied up, one table was ready first with all the children sitting beautifully around their immaculate table. With the time nearly up, one child from this table leapt up and picked up a pencil from the middle of the carpet area and put it away, risking his table's point. You could see from the annoyed faces of the other children on his table they were not happy!

They didn't want to lose their hard earned point but once I'd awarded points to each table, I gave an extra class point because this child had taken responsibility for outside his designated area to make sure the whole class was tidy; he was a hero that day! He had demonstrated a behaviour I wanted to encourage; for the children to take responsibility for their whole environment. It was a small act but significant enough to show desirable behaviour.

From then on my class looked a lot further when they were tidying their tables.

This is a something you can certainly start with your leadership team but it's also something you do with the wider team. What do they think these core values look like when they're being demonstrated around the school by children and adults?

Step 2: Tell them where

Next, tell people where you are taking your school. Think about the school you want to create, what will it look like, what will people be saying and doing? What kind of results will you get? How will the children have developed when they leave you? What will children say about the school when they come back to visit, or when they are adults?

ACTIVITY

Daydream about the school and education you want to create, make notes, draw pictures, whatever lets you capture what is in your head. I know you became a Head for a reason, so now's your time to get that out of your brain and share it, unashamedly. Pick a nice time and space to do this and enjoy it!

Step 3: Tell them

How you share your vision is as important as the vision itself. Your daydream of your ideal school provides the content for your vision; however we need to shape this so that people can remember it easily without having to chant it!

A school I worked with had spent a lot of time developing their vision, with staff, Governors and parents, and one of the team, who had attended all of the sessions, said to me 'You know, I helped write that and I can't even remember it; it's just words!'

So we developed their vision into something more meaningful, a story about the day in the life of the school and what you would see when you walked around, a vision which stirred emotion and created images in everyone's mind.

You see we don't remember lists very easily (that's why we write them down) but we can all remember an evocative story. When you regale friends with amusing stories about your weekend, your children or your holiday, you don't need to write them down to remember do you? So when you are communicating your vision use stories. Our brains love them!

I've always been impressed by the creativity of school leaders when creating a heart-warming vision and this example from the senior leadership team at Capel Manor School in Enfield is a delightful example of the power of story and the emotional connection a vision should stir.

BONUS MATERIAL

You can see more examples online at *www.ukheadsup. com/free-resources/creating-a-great-vision/case-studies- vision/*

The making of Joseph Martin

Dear Diary,

My little baby, Joseph, started school today. Boy was he nervous! He wouldnt let go of my leg and the worry was etched on his little face!

Susan

Merry christmas Mum & Dad,

Our Joseph is a proper little man now. He loves school, has lots of friends and is reading and writing a bit too!

Love Simon, Susan & Joseph xxx

Capel Manor Year 6 Personal Comment

As Joseph leaves Capel Manor, I am extremely proud of the young man he has become. He is respectful, kind and is not afraid to stand up for what he believes in. He says he wants to be a vet, and I truly believe he will be!

Miss Cannon

Year 11 Presentation Evening

"As Head teacher of Lee Valley High School, it is with great honour to open this presentation evening which showcases out pupil's successes. And our first award, the community award, goes to *Joseph Martin* for his dedication and service to the Enfield Dog Rescue Centre."

Dear UCAS,

My name is Joseph Martin and I would like to be considered for the veterinary course at the Royal Veterinary College.

As I enter adulthood, I look back upon my life experiences which have brought me to this point and I know the skills I have learnt will take me far in life.

My parents and first school years gave me confidence, independence and made me resilient. Teachers inspired me to develop a true love for learning.

My voluntary work at the Enfield Dog Rescue Centre and my passion for science has motivated me through the years to become a successful qualified vet.

I am a hard-working individual who, I know, can make a difference to the life of animals.

Yours sincerely,

Joseph Martin

Every vision has a unique message and delivery. Your vision might be told like Capel Manor's as a story, but even if it's not you can still incorporate stories. One school I worked with had the vision 'To unlock the doors of opportunity for our children' and when they shared this vision they used stories of past pupils and how they had unlocked their doors, as well as stories of current pupils and what unlocking their doors might be for them: gifted children, those with special needs and others in between. It was so compelling that when the Head shared it she received a heartfelt round of applause!

ACTIVITY

Take the daydream you had about the school you want to create and put it into words, that might be a sentence, but it might be a paragraph, like 'a day in the life of', or some other story.

A FEW TRAPS TO WATCH OUT FOR WHEN CRAFTING YOUR VISION

The difference between a motto and vision

A motto is a short, often snappy, phrase such as:

John Lewis – Never knowingly undersold
Tesco – Every little helps
Nike – Just do it

Every child matters
Love learning every day
Secondary ready

There is a place for mottos, without a doubt, but they do not do the job of a vision. What mottos do is give us a quick way of remembering our direction, so Tesco's motto is a short cut to knowing what Tesco is about but it doesn't tell us specifically what is being helped.

Every little penny saved helps?

Every little piece of customer service helps for a nicer shopping experience?

Every little piece of quality product helps our customers live better?

It might be all of the above, none, or some and this where vision comes in: vision creates clarity for the team to know exactly what they are striving for. But even the three more explicit statements above don't go far enough because they are unlikely to motivate the team.

The difference between vision and mission

Vision and mission are different; a vision is why you are doing what you are doing and your mission is how you will do that. For example, I believe education is the key to creating a greater society, so my vision is societal, it's about improving society.

This is the reason I do what I do and what I do is my mission: to make all schools outstanding because I believe education is the key to that future and superb education, in the fullest sense of the word, provides children with the best start in life to create that greater society.

The way I do this is by working with Heads and school leaders who want to deliver exceptional education and I help them create a high performing culture.

But my mission doesn't have to be obviously linked to my vision. My vision is to improve society by resolving the issues that exist today. I could work at this in many ways: I could try to get laws passed to force people to behave in ways that would improve society, I could try to tackle existing health problems by working to have cigarettes, alcohol and processed foods banned and I could lobby for more police to reduce crime. I choose to focus on education, that is my mission, but it doesn't have to be in order to work toward my vision. An example from a school is:

Vision	We believe education is the most powerful gift
Mission	To be green (on a range of in-school targets)

They could achieve their vision in many other ways, like build schools in developing countries or develop online lessons for a global audience, but they choose to deliver excellent education, shown by meeting important targets, in their community.

Fundamentally a vision doesn't change; it's your belief and driver for doing what you do. You might shape it, develop it and communicate it better or in different ways but the core vision tends to remain the same. Your vision should be unachievable, that's its power. Your mission is how you choose to make that vision a reality and should be achievable, it might take a long time, but it should have the potential to be 'ticked off' the list.

In the school 'To be green' they know exactly what they need to do to achieve their mission, and it's a nice easy way to keep everyone focused.

ACTIVITY

Now take your vision and craft your mission: What will you actually do? Remember this is one primary objective and you should potentially be able to tick it off the list one day.

Step 4: Tell them how you will create that school

If your values resonate with the team they will be beginning to get on your bus (if they're not already), if the picture of where you are going excites them so much that they want to be part of creating that, then they are pretty much on your bus, and to give them everything they need to be fully on (or off) your bus you need to tell them how you will get to that destination.

The strategic triangle

Creating the plan, in particular the objectives and tactics, is the place most schools, in fact most organisations, start; the great ones start with their vision and then everything they do is pointed towards that. Every time they review and amend their plan it's always with the vision at the forefront of their mind.

The diagram on the next page shows how your vision, mission and plan all fit together:

Figure 9: The strategic triangle.

As we move down the triangle the frequency of change increases. As I've said your vision is likely to remain fixed, your mission might take years or decades to achieve, however strategy, objectives and tactics will change far more regularly, on a termly or even weekly basis. Your vision is your guiding star, keeping you on track.

What goes into the plan: BAU vs development

There are things you will do in school that are business as usual (BAU) tasks such as maintain the building, lesson observations, even child protection. These are things that work when they need to, they don't require specific focus and energy, or an improvement drive, they just happen as they should.

If you think about your day to day life there are actions you do not need to write on a daily list: brush teeth, get dressed, make lunch etc. These are tasks that just happen automatically as part of your routine.

However there are areas in school that we decide to drive forward: these are development areas. So you might have a drive to improve boys writing, or phonics, or the outdoor early years' areas. In the analogy of your life, 'developments' might be starting a family, moving house, planning a big holiday, doing a Masters or a sporting achievement.

ACTIVITY

With your mission in hand, what are the key development areas you need to drive forward to move closer to achieving your mission and vision? This is definitely a place where less is more so pick no more than five.

It might be you want to focus solely on moving teaching to outstanding across the school, that you want to develop the school's middle leaders, that you want to increase experiential learning; there are countless areas.

When choosing make sure you keep a steady eye on your vision and mission and choose the areas that help you move toward it the fastest.

Step 5: Keep your vision alive

A lot of schools struggle to remember their vision. This tells me that either their vision isn't compelling, isn't communicated well or that it's been so long since anyone talked about it they can't remember it.

The trick with really embedding a vision is to not make it a 'once a year' event. Yes of course you will want to re-visit it during your September IN-SErvice Training (INSET), but you have to talk about vision and values on a daily basis, just like when you were a class teacher. Then it will become a part of your school's DNA.

Talk about the vision in relation to school plans and refer to the vision in performance management meetings. Most schools have their vision on a wall in the school entrance, on their website and school prospectus. This keeps in mind that you're aiming for your vision to become a way of life.

One way you know your vision is becoming embedded in your school is when your team starts to either challenge actions that don't seem to contribute to the vision or come up with ideas to support it.

Your vision is your school's guiding star.

CHAPTER SUMMARY

- *Vision is a necessary courtesy of leadership letting people choose to be on your bus*
- *A vision is not a mission or a motto and must be based in values*
- *Getting clear on our vision is hard because it lives in an inarticulate part of our brain*
- *We need to talk to peoples limbic system when we talk about our vision*
- *Talk about your vision daily*

Chapter 6
Creating a culture of healthy conflict through successful difficult conversations

'Peace is not absence of conflict, it is the ability
to handle conflict by peaceful means.'
Ronald Reagan

In this chapter:
- *Why you must have successful difficult conversations if you want high performance*
- *Making sure you've got good foundations in place so you can tackle issues*
- *How to have successful difficult conversations about performance and behaviour*

THE KEY TO HIGH PERFORMANCE IS MANAGING CONFLICT EFFECTIVELY

If you were to use only one of the three key leadership strategies that create an outstanding culture having successful difficult conversations should be the one you pick; it will make the biggest overall difference to your culture.

Think about an average week in school. How often do you find yourself having a difficult conversation? Most people tell me it's a daily occurrence. It might be someone coming to you about an issue or you might have to talk to a member of staff or parent about something tricky.

Difficult conversations are a fundamental part of leadership and as a Head the buck stops with you. Yet, despite the fact difficult conversations are a daily occurrence for leaders, very few leaders are trained in how to have them successfully.

What's more, healthy conflict is a key feature of high performing teams so it's perplexing that more support isn't given in developing this skill.

GREAT LEADERS BUILD HONEST PROFESSIONAL RELATIONSHIPS

They tackle performance issues

Great leaders are aware of and tackle staff issues quickly. If performance of a team or team member isn't meeting expectations then effective leaders deal with this promptly and in the right way. Staff should have clearly defined outcomes and timescales and excellent support in place to help them improve (which is the ideal outcome), and if they don't improve then, with sadness, they might have to leave. I don't say this lightly and it is my least preferred option. One of the main reasons I'm so passionate about successful difficult conversations is I don't want anyone to have to leave their job, but I also want children to receive the best quality education. I'm sure you feel the same. I believe if you have the difficult conversations early enough it's far easier to get staff back on track.

They tackle poor adult behaviour

Effective leaders not only tackle performance issues but they also tackle the behaviour of staff, they can do this because they are so clear about what behaviour is expected from their team. **Every organisation has a culture and culture is the combination of how people behave within it, so the behaviour of adults is crucial to any organisation (just as the behaviour of children is crucial to a class).**

Constructive, honest and professional relationships

Healthy relationships are about having no unresolved issues, grudges or misunderstandings.

If a member of your team is often late to meetings and then spends the first five minutes rummaging in their handbag instead of giving her full attention to the meeting, which had now been delayed by five minutes, as a Head I worked with once told me, this 'niggle' needs to be addressed. It's not a full-on disciplinary issue, it's a conversation about inconsiderate behaviour and its impact on the team.

This may seem like a small irritation but over time these small issues accumulate and eventually reach a breaking point and built-up resentment is unleashed on the 'culprit'.

I say 'culprit' because often the person is unaware of the full impact of their behaviour and so it can be a shock to them when they find out and something they could have change had they known.

Nip these niggles in the bud as early as possible and avoid having to have a very difficult conversation later on; be fair to the other person in letting them know in a timely fashion and develop a constructive, honest professional relationship. The more you do this, the more normal having these conversations becomes and you will build up both of your own and others' abilities to have a successful difficult conversation, and resolve future issues with greater ease and success.

BEHAVIOUR VS PERFORMANCE

As a teacher did you talk to your class more about their performance or their behaviour? My guess is you spoke more about behaviour, from being nice to one another, to learning behaviours, to how they behave as a class team. With the staff in your school do you talk more about their performance or their behaviour? **I find we are more willing to talk to adults about performance than behaviour.** Why is that?

I think it's because performance feels less personal than talking to someone about their behaviour.

However behaviour is not about personality, it's a choice and can be adjusted. Yet it's something most of us are more comfortable talking to children about rather than adults.

Behaviour breeds behaviour

Behaviour is a bit like a game of tennis. I demonstrate a behaviour (hit the ball) and you react to it, and then I will react to your response (return of the ball) and so on. We cannot change someone else's behaviour but we can change our own. Some adult behaviour issues are pretty obvious; however some are more subtle.

Do you have a member of staff who wears their 'special face' (you know what I mean) in staff meetings or during assemblies? Do you have someone who is rude but says it's because they are honest and speak their mind? All of these behaviours have a knock on effect to others because behaviour breeds behaviour (like a volley in a tennis match!).

A great example of behaviour breeding behaviour was with a Deputy Head having a difficult conversation with a teacher. This teacher wouldn't talk to anyone else on the leadership team about the performance and personal issues she was having, only the Deputy, and when role playing the conversation it became pretty clear as to why.

The Deputy's behaviour became very mothering, to the point of smothering; she was so concerned and caring that the teacher became like a child asking for her mother's help. I'm all for caring for each other but this was extreme and unhelpful because it was stopping the teacher from moving forward.

With the Deputy changing how she behaved, ever so slightly, she still showed care but in a more adult way and the progress she was able to make significantly improved.

The Deputy's behaviour bred the teacher's behaviour. Or maybe it was the other way around? To be honest it doesn't matter who 'started it', the fact remains that a behaviour bred another behaviour and the cycle continued until one of them changed.

IT'S NATURAL TO WANT TO AVOID DIFFICULT CONVERSATIONS

Almost everyone avoids difficult conversations and when you do have these conversations it would be normal for you to dread them. There are several reasons for this:

1. We don't want to upset the other person or upset ourselves, which is understandable.

2. We think the problem might resolve itself by giving it time (which is sometimes true).

3. It's an anxiety-inducing situation to give someone a difficult message or discuss a difficult topic and no-one likes feeling anxious.

I also think we are not taught how to have these conversations effectively nor why they are important to master.

Here are some 'excuses' we all make (myself included!):

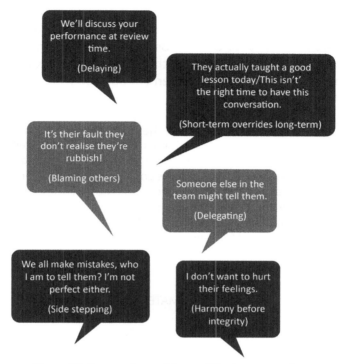

Figure 10: Excuses for avoiding a difficult conversation

Now imagine applying these excuses to children:

• I don't want to hurt their feelings, so I won't tell them they were mean to another child/that they are capable of better work.

• We'll discuss their performance at parent's evening next month rather than discuss their work today.

• Some other teacher might tell them.

These 'reasons' are bizarre when applied to children and yet we use them with adults all the time.

We need to talk to adults about their behaviour more, just like we do with children, because, I don't know about you, but my behaviour isn't always as good as I'd like and I rely on those nearest and dearest to help me understand when I'm adversely affecting them so I can improve.

After working with a Head he understood how he could speak to his team about their behaviour as well performance. He had a really constructive conversation with a member of staff who was considered 'a bit of bitch': she was negative, no-one got along with her and the Head, like pretty much everyone else, struggled to work with her. They had a constructive conversation where she shared her thoughts and feelings and they completely turned the situation around.

BONUS MATERIAL

You're not alone with your difficult conversations and you can read how Heads have turned theirs around at *www.ukheadsup.com/free-resources/improve-difficult-conversations/case-studies-dc/*

Consider the consequences of not having the conversation

Whenever you're questioning if you should or shouldn't have a difficult conversation consider the consequences of not having it. This is something I'm passionate about in all aspects of life because ultimately I want people to be happy but I see people suffer stress and anxiety due to their relationships, both personal and professional. It might be an over-protective mother whom smoothers their 41-year-old son, it might be a boss who is abrupt to a team member but doesn't realise the impact, it might be an under-performing teacher who can't muster the courage to seek help.

All of these situations bring some form of stress and although dealing with these issues is uncomfortable, it sets you on the path to removing that stress.

So the choice we're faced with is:

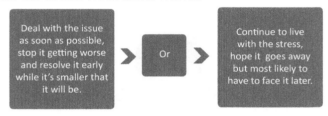

Figure 11: When deciding to have a difficult conversation or not we are making a choice between keeping a stress in our lives or giving ourselves the chance to remove it

Imagine that for every issue you have with someone, big or small, for each stress in your life, you pick up a rock and put it in a rucksack on your back. Keep doing this for every person and every issue and it wouldn't take long before that rucksack begins to weigh you down. In having successful difficult conversations you will have less rocks in your rucksack, ultimately none, so that when a rock comes along you can hold it in your hand, deal with it, and then put it down.

The most useful theory about why we need to have difficult conversations

There are many theories and models about team dynamics but I find the Theory of Group Formation (Tuckman, 1965) most useful.

You might know it better as 'forming, storming, norming and performing'. Let me take you through the theory, which can be seen at work as soon as you have two or more people engaged in an on-going relationship (romantic, professional, friendship or otherwise).

Figure 12: Tuckman's (1965) theory of group formation

Forming

When a group or team forms, they go through a 'getting to know you' phase called *forming*. Conversation centres around factual information to build a picture of each person, for example:

'Where do you live?'
'How many children do you have?
How old are they?'
'Oh I have cats too! Have you always had cats?'

There is a giving and receiving of information and people tend to be on their best behaviour, wanting to fit in and make a good impression. This is like the honeymoon period of a new romance.

Storming

But the honeymoon ends and *storming* begins. This is when the team start to test the metaphorical boundaries of the team:

Is it ok to be late?
Do we swear?
What if I don't do that bit of work on time?

People rarely ask this explicitly and it's not always conscious. They often try things and see how the team or leader reacts. They also observe what others do and use that to help understand where the lines are drawn. If someone else in the team swears and it's okay then it seems fair to say that I can swear and it should be okay – it's what we can do in this team.

During this stage disagreements start to appear because these boundaries are being tested and people might 'over step the mark'. It's also a time when people might start to try and position themselves in the team. For example a senior leader of many years might feel they are more important in the group and start to jostle for top position, perhaps overriding or undermining decisions or ideas of others.

It's a tricky and uncomfortable time for teams where people often think: 'We were we getting on so well and now we're not, what's gone wrong?'

Norming

Once the team has stormed they will have established some norms, hopefully *good norms*, of how their team behaves and works. It might be that we don't swear and being late is not acceptable; these are good norms. It might be that one team member gets upset easily so the team softens things for them, or another team member is rude and confrontational but the rest of the team accepts 'that's just the way they are'; these are *bad norms*.

Performing

Once the team has *normed* they are ready to really start performing. This doesn't mean they haven't performed and delivered results up to this point. Work doesn't go on hold for team dynamics because work is the context around which this team dynamics form.

But now they can settle because many of the team dynamics have been established and energy can be more focused on work. In school you have a clear example of this theory in operation.

The best example of Tuckman's theory at work: The school year

Every September class teachers are faced with a new group of children, so they enter the *forming* stage. During the month of September the class and teacher get to know each other, and generally the children are pretty well behaved because they want to impress their new teacher. However towards the October half term behaviour seems to become more challenging because we are moving into the *storming* stage. Children are testing the strength of those metaphorical lines.

They are 'metaphorical' lines because the teacher and the school will have set up expectations for behaviour and set class rules. It's likely these were the same rules the class had the previous year however these are just words! In storming we test how much these rules are really adhered to and we test codes of behaviour that haven't been explicitly stated.

So when the teacher says 'silent reading' does she really mean complete silence or can I whisper to the person next to me? Or can I draw pictures as long as I'm silent? The way a child finds out depends on the reaction of the teacher; if they are strict then 'silent reading' means being quiet while reading and the whole class observes the teacher raise this with a pupil who isn't complying. I'm sure you can think of many more examples of the unspoken rules in class which children test.

The belief that children like strict teachers is a misleading. What they actually like, as do adults, is knowing where the lines are drawn. The lines might be tight (strict) or wide (less strict) but they are clear and consistently applied.

Storming tends to continue through the autumn term and then December comes and Christmas, glitter, nativities and carol singing take over.

Returning to school in January the class has usually settled; they know how their teacher works, they know the lines that are different in this class to their previous class and they are able to work within them; they have *normed*. Every now and then they will test them again and some children will find it harder to stick within those lines, but overall the class has settled and January feels quite different to the autumn term.

I don't know about you but I think the spring term is the engine room of the school year, class behaviour has settled and now the class can really get on with the job of learning. Teachers have been teaching and the children learning ever since September but now it's easier and better. The class, the team, are able to *perform* at a higher level.

Does that sound familiar? You might also think of a time when you had a new staff member join your team and the same process occurred. It also happens when teams are suddenly put into a new context such as a school amalgamation or new build; they will often go through this process again, perhaps a little faster because they already understand their team but the new context throws up new ways of operating, which they need to adjust to.

One stage is more important than all others.

The importance of storming

The most important part of the Tuckman's group formation cycle is storming. A group that storms well, by understanding boundaries and their roles in the team with an ability to air issues as they arise, has the potential to become a high performing team. During their storming they will have established good norms.

Without effective storming and effective on-going *storming* (because fresh issues arise as time goes by) a team will struggle to meet its full potential. So how can you *storm* better?

Firstly, *storming* is not about arguing. The art of *storming* is fostering healthy conflict, which helps move relationships and the team forward by addressing issues quickly. This can be easier in the classroom because of the obvious hierarchy with the class teacher as the leader of the group. However *storming* is harder when working with peers and superiors. If the leader always 'sorts out' the issue, there isn't a culture of healthy conflict resolution between peers. Dealing with conflict, *storming*, can be learnt and is essential for effective relationships, personally and professionally.

I love sharing Tuckman's theory with school teams because they are quickly able to see where their team is functioning and often they gain insight around storming. Maybe the team is currently going through a stormy patch! Knowing this is a natural part of their cycle makes it instantly easier, or perhaps they realise they have not stormed as well as they needed to.

I worked with a leadership team that ran two schools; the deputy head said to me 'You mean it's okay to disagree? In fact, we should if there's an issue?' And my answer was 'Yes'. Now this needs to be done in the right way, as I said storming is not about arguing or shouting but about creative discussion that reaches the best solution together.

This particular deputy talked to his Head who decided not to attend the training days so the team could speak more freely and have some healthy conflict! They sat down and aired key issues effectively and as a result strengthened mutual respect. The next time I saw the Deputy he looked an inch taller and the leadership team noticed the difference in him since the healthy conflict with his Head.

THE IMPLICATIONS FOR YOU AND YOUR TEAM

Tuckman's theory applies to all relationships, professional and personal: in a new romance all is blissful, then after the honeymoon period, arguments erupt, but if the couple can get past the rocky patch, they norm and hopefully have a wonderful relationship.

All teams go through this process and what varies is how well a team progresses through the stages.

I rarely come across an organisation (school or other) where *storming* has happened to the extent it needs to.

Teams can get stuck as they progress, some never break out of *storming*, others don't *storm* well enough so although they move on to *norm* and *perform* they are constantly held back by the lack of effective *storming* with entrenched *bad norms*. Some will *norm* with distorted behaviours that prevent them from achieving high performance.

I worked with a very good school leadership team that had the potential to be high performing, except they had one member of staff who was brilliant at her job but awful in her behaviour with the team.

She was rude, aggressive, sometimes passive-aggressive, which meant the team walked on egg shells and, to an extent, cowered around her, even the Head I'm sorry to say. She was excellent at her job but her behaviour was stopping the team from realising its potential. They hadn't stormed well and had adopted bad norms by allowing her to continue with aggressive behaviour.

The right thing was to talk to her, which was hard because she was, to put it simply, a scary lady, but a scary lady who clearly cared, otherwise she wouldn't have done her job so well.

ACTIVITY

Take a moment to think about the following:

- *Is there anyone in your team who doesn't behave as you would expect in a professional environment?*
- *Is there a rude person?*

- *An aggressive person?*
- *Someone who is passive-aggressive?*
- *Someone who stirs things up?*
- *Someone you have to 'manage' more than others?*
- *Someone who wears their 'special face' in staff meetings or assemblies?*
- *Anyone who is regularly negative and not constructive?*
- *Someone who thinks that school rules or initiatives don't apply to them?*
- *Anyone who intimidates others because they might shout or get angry with them?*
- *Anyone who others worry about upsetting because they are likely to cry?*
- *Anyone you think is lazy?*
- *Anyone you don't trust?*

These questions are focused on people but it's not about the person it's about the behaviour they are demonstrating. These questions are focused on behaviour, not performance, because behaviour creates culture.

If any of those statements ring true you are not alone, in fact you have a lot of company as you could walk into almost every school and organisation in the country and find that some of these statements are true. But I believe you want to deliver exceptional education and a big part of that, one of the three key leadership strategies, is tackling under-performance and poor adult behaviour so that you create a high performing team.

HAVING SUCCESSFUL
DIFFICULT CONVERSATIONS

When tackling under-performance or staff behaviour there are a few steps you need to take that will permeate positively throughout your culture.

Step 1: Clear expectations

Expectations of performance

In tackling under-performance, long before it becomes a capability issue, you need to set expectations for performance. The Teacher Standards are a good starting place but I feel they are not explicit enough.

The best Heads I've met are really clear about what they expect from their teachers, for example, Am Rai and his team at Montpelier Primary School achieved an *Outstanding* rating in 2012. When it comes to his teaching staff he expects one thing and one thing only: to teach outstanding lessons. To support this teachers don't have break duty and are not expected to run after school clubs: they are to focus only on being outstanding classroom teachers. With such clear direction backed up with these actions it's not surprising that the Ofsted report said:

'Achievement is outstanding because pupils' attainment is well-above average and the pupils make excellent progress in their learning at all stages of their education.

They also progress very well in areas other than the strictly academic, in their social, moral, spiritual, and cultural development, in their enthusiastic take up of the school's many extra-curricular activities, and in their development as mature, reflective and articulate young people.

Teaching is excellent throughout the school. Pupils say that this is because 'teachers make learning more fun by making lessons more fun'. Parents and carers agree. In the words of one parent, 'my child adores her teachers.'"

Be outstanding teachers. That is a very clear expectation.

It doesn't mean he puts them into capability the moment they have a good, but not outstanding, lesson, but it does allow the conversation to be very much focused on how to get back up to outstanding and not accept good is 'good enough'. Consistency is so important in leadership. You must be consistent in expecting the same high standards from everyone.

Now you might be thinking 'But what about Newly Qualified Teachers (NQT)? I can't expect them to be outstanding in their first year!' And you might be right, but you can expect them to be outstanding within a time frame, even if it's two years later, and support them to get there. What an exciting stretch for an NQT to know their school wants them to be outstanding in their third year of teaching and will work closely with them to get them there. Talk about developing your team! But it also places an expectation on the NQT to do their part by giving a clear goal, crystallised by observing outstanding teachers and their lessons, demonstrating the kind of quality they are aspiring to achieve.

As much as I'm a fan of consistency and think it's important in leadership, the trick with consistency is to apply it broadly and know when not to. So if someone is having difficulties in their home life you might accept a dip in their performance for the moment with an expectation that it improves when those troubles are resolved.

Expectations of behaviour

I don't think we discuss adult behaviour enough but expectations are set out in the teacher standards and here are some excerpts:

- A teacher is expected to demonstrate consistently high standards of personal and professional conduct.
- Teachers must have proper and professional regard for the ethos, policies and practices of the school in which they teach, and maintain high standards in their own attendance and punctuality.
- Make a positive contribution to the wider life and ethos of the school.
- Develop effective professional relationships with colleagues, knowing how and when to draw on advice and specialist support .
- Take responsibility for improving teaching through appropriate professional development, responding to advice and feedback from colleagues.

Taken from DFEE Teachers' Standards Guidance for school leaders, school staff & governing bodies (Department for Education, 2013)

But these guidelines are like those wordy visions mentioned earlier; they don't create a clear picture that would let staff understand clearly your expectations of behaviour.

You will have in your own mind your expectations of your team and need to make this really clear, just as you would as a class teacher, so your team have a good chance of meeting them.

ACTIVITY

Create an avatar.

This is a nice activity that you can do on your own, or with your leadership or wider team to create an avatar whom embodies the behaviour and performance you expect of the adults in your school.

This avatar is a representation of the kind of person you want in a role in your school. To do this you might think of a teacher, either one who embodies everything you want in a teacher, or perhaps a few teachers who have components of what you want. Write down what it is they do. Try to keep this really concrete and not abstract, for example:

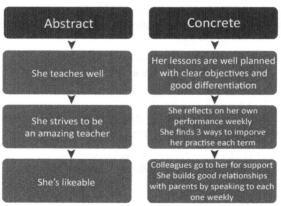

Figure 13: Concrete versus abstract language

Be really thorough in describing what you mean and then review your notes to make sure you have been as concrete as possible.

You can create one for all roles in the school, for example, who is your ideal teacher/TA/site manager/office staff, even your own role. This doesn't mean you will have clones or teachers with the same level of experience. What you are looking for are traits like attitude, approach and resilience, characteristics that someone in this role will display.

Step 2: Make sure your house is in order

This might seem dull but it really is about laying solid foundations so you don't come a cropper later. If your difficult conversations lead to capability and tribunal you want to be in the strongest position, morally and legally, ensuring that you were genuinely fair to the person and within the law. The best advice for leaders when tackling staff issues is to always think you will go to tribunal. It's far better to have made unnecessary records, checked policies and consulted your Human Resource (HR) advisors than to find yourself at tribunal with a judge asking for these documents.

I am not an employment lawyer or a HR advisor but as a leader, and in my work with both lawyers and schools, some things are clearly good practice.

Check your policies

Make sure your policies are right and you are familiar with them. Capability procedures changed; does your policy reflect this? Are you using the National Union of Teachers (NUT) recommended policy, the Department for Education (DFE) policy or another one and if so why?

Particularly with the capability policy do not wait until you are in a capability process to check this, if you've not looked at it for a while or you know there are issues you will be tackling soon make sure the policy is fit for purpose and within the law. Make sure your team have up to date copies.

I've heard stories from NUT reps where staff are handed a copy of the new capability policy as they walk into their first capability meeting. This is just not fair on the staff member involved. I'm sure it wasn't the Head's intention to spring this surprise. Perhaps they only realised the old policy was outdated close to the meeting, but it's still not fair on that person.

It's also worth checking your *Disciplinary* and *Grievance* policy and *Pay* policy as well. I know this kind of work is tedious and so if you have the resources to get a professional to check your policies or provide updates then it can be a less onerous way of ensuring your policies are fit for purpose.

You must make sure that you are familiar with the policy. Many issues come from the application of the policy more so than the policy itself so make sure you understand the policy and what it means for you and your staff when you are using it.

If you do need to change a policy make sure you follow the correct procedure and make sure staff have a copy.

Clarity of roles

This relates to expectations of performance and behaviour covered earlier; all staff members need to be clear about their roles.

This sounds straightforward enough but in schools roles can often morph into bespoke roles, which are only found in that school. This is fine and it is up to you to decide what roles are required but make sure there is a job description, or something which explains any additional responsibility, and have them all in one place so you can easily check anytime a change is being made.

This is a good exercise for the head teacher to do because it means you are really clear about each role and what outcomes you want; and the clearer you are the more likely the person will deliver. If you ever have a re-structure such documents are invaluable.

When I worked in business I moved to Head Office to run a team of senior managers. One of the first things I did was review their Job Descriptions (JDs) because they would be working toward key deliverables. I wanted to make sure these matched their JDs. I found that several roles, which were the same in practice, all had very different job descriptions and deliverables.

With HR advice and in consultation with my team we re-shaped the roles to be an accurate reflection of what was actually required and made them the same across the team.

In total it was no more than two hours of work for me and less for the others involved.

Then 18 months later there was, as is so common in business, a review of our teams and a mild panic set in amongst the managers and HR who realised they needed to check that their team's job descriptions were accurate. This would affect eligibility for redundancy and job transfers.

Because we had updated my team's roles the review was easier on them during this uncertain time because their roles were accurately reflected in their job descriptions.

It's likely your teachers are clearer on expectations than others as there are more supporting documents for this role, but what about your leadership roles, admin staff, teaching assistants, site manager, learning mentors, higher level teaching assistants, mid-day supervisors, Governors and anyone else in your team? Are their JD's all in one place and do they all accurately reflect what you expect from someone in that role? Do they tell people both the behaviour and performance expectations? Do they set out their responsibilities? And their deliverables? It's worth checking they do because if you need to tackle an issue or hold them to account the JD is an important foundation.

If you need to update or change a job description speak to your HR support so amendments are done correctly.

With performance-related pay in schools JD's are even more important to you and your staff because they tell people the expectations for their role, which your pay band descriptors clarify further.

Make sure you have human resource support

Whether you call it human resources or personnel you probably have someone in place to call on to give you good advice. Keep in close contact with them as you tackle issues because a good HR advisor will make sure you're going about procedure in the correct legal way. If you're not happy with your HR support then you might want to explore consultancy services.

Step 3: Identify where the issues are

You are tackling staff issues because you want to create a high performing team that can deliver the best education possible and create the school you dream of leading. **Tackling staff issues is part of culture change and is a crucial part of this process.** Initially you need to be clear in your own mind where the key issues lay. And while there might be several trouble spots you need to prioritise because of limited time and resources.

ACTIVITY

With your leadership team, take various groups (such as teachers, TAs, admin staff, Governors) and discuss who is:

1. Not performing to expectations
2. Not behaving to expectations

Once you have this list arrange them into a priority order with those having the biggest detrimental impact at the top; this will tell you who to focus on first.

Step 4: Have successful difficult conversations about performance or behaviour

In life we all need to have difficult conversations and we can usually avoid at least some of them or at the very least postpone them. The same is true for you as a leader. **In leadership your ability to have difficult conversations is really a test of your leadership mettle.** I would say it's a test of character in life as well and mastering this skill can create far happier relationships and less stress. However it's an optional skill in your personal life but a necessary skill in your role as leader.

THERE ARE THREE ELEMENTS TO HAVING A SUCCESSFUL DIFFICULT CONVERSATION

To have a successful difficult conversation you need to:
1. Build trust.
2. Manage emotions (yours and theirs).
3. Structure the conversation.

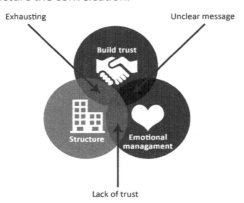

Figure 14: The three elements needed to have a successful difficult conversation

It's not enough to have only two of these variables in place, let's look at why:

1. If you have trust and manage emotions but have *no structure* – the conversation lacks focus and is not likely to lead to change.

   Ever felt like the other person didn't get your point?

2. If you have trust and structure but *don't manage the emotions* – the conversation is exhausting and you are both likely to be *mentally chewing* on it afterwards.

   Ever gone home and relived, replayed or re-invented the conversation?

3. If you manage the emotions and structure the conversation but *don't have trust* – it can lead to resentment. Any conversation where there is little trust is unlikely to be successful.

   Ever thought 'They're clearly not going to do what I've asked them to'?

Part 1: Build trust

The first part of any difficult conversation, if it is to be successful, is to build trust. Remember the limbic system covered earlier? Well building trust is about letting this part of the brain feel as safe as possible in the other person. I'm sure you're familiar with the phrase 'It's not what you say it's how you say it'.

Psychologist Dr Albert Mehrabian has shown that non-verbal body language and facial expressions count far more than words.

It's important to note that his research focused on how we communicate feelings and attitudes because his findings have been widely over-generalised. He found:

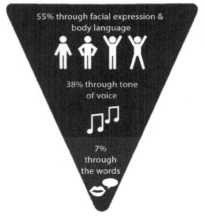

Figure 15: The split of non-verbal and verbal communication when communicating attitudes and feelings (Mehrabian, 1964)

So what can we do about our non-verbal communication? There are times when your non-verbal communication is effortlessly positive and congruent when you are with people you like and get on with, your communication is encouraging, trusting and safe. 'Safe' is the keyword here. The fact you do this with those you like, without thinking about it, shows that you are capable of creating this safe space and building trust.

In successful difficult conversations making the interaction safe is a key component. Without emotional safety it's unlikely the conversation will progress well. The key skill required to master difficult conversations is rapport, something you already use with close friends.

Developing your skills to quickly build trust

'Rapport is the ability to enter someone else's world, to make him feel that you understand him, that you have a strong common bond.'
Tony Robbins, coach and motivational speaker.

Building trust is really about building rapport to create a safe interaction, so you are both more likely to be heard and open up and tackle the issue together. The good news is, building rapport is easy!

To create rapport you need to behave like a mirror. You want to imitate the other person, not in an overt way, but subtly. Sit like they do and use their words and gestures; remember we do this naturally with people we like and trust.

ACTIVITY

Start to look for examples of rapport in your daily life, on TV, in photographs and magazines; you'll see it when people are feeling the same way.

Start to notice when you are mirroring and don't break rapport; it's a wonderful non-verbal signal to someone that you like them and feel comfortable and safe with them.

Next time you're in a difficult conversation simply sit like the other person. The change in body language seems minor and yet it has a powerful effect. If you can use their words and phrases you'll build even more trust.

Questioning and listening to build trust

A lot of people will say phrases like 'I hear you...', 'I'm listening to you ...' when sadly they often are not or even worse they are only hearing what they want to hear.

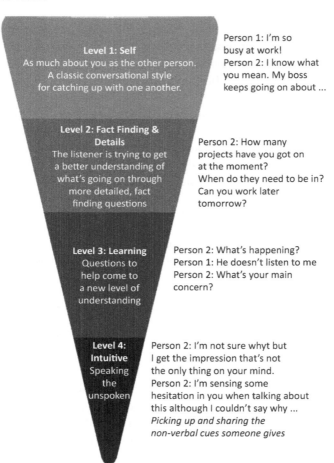

Level 1: Self
As much about you as the other person. A classic conversational style for catching up with one another.

Person 1: I'm so busy at work!
Person 2: I know what you mean. My boss keeps going on about ...

Level 2: Fact Finding & Details
The listener is trying to get a better understanding of what's going on through more detailed, fact finding questions

Person 2: How many projects have you got on at the moment?
When do they need to be in?
Can you work later tomorrow?

Level 3: Learning
Questions to help come to a new level of understanding

Person 2: What's happening?
Person 1: He doesn't listen to me
Person 2: What's your main concern?

Level 4: Intuitive
Speaking the unspoken

Person 2: I'm not sure whyt but I get the impression that's not the only thing on your mind.
Person 2: I'm sensing some hesitation in you when talking about this although I couldn't say why ...
Picking up and sharing the non-verbal cues someone gives

Figure 16: Question & listening triangle

Have you ever had a conversation with someone to find out later they understood something different to what you meant? If we truly listen to someone we are receptive to finding out more about the situation and the other person's perspective and ultimately stand a better chance of having a successful difficult conversation.

Figure 16 shows deeper levels of questioning and listening. Working your way toward the deeper levels of questioning and listening will help you tackle the core issues. Levels 1 and 2 are information and fact exchanges which often only deal with surface issues. Level 3 aims to create learning and insight. You'll know if you've asked a learning question because the other person will need to think about their answer. And level 4 is about sharing what you are seeing in someone's non-verbal behaviour.

Part 2: Emotional management

One of the hardest parts of a difficult conversation is managing yourself while in the conversation and after the conversation. Ever gone home replaying the conversation in your head? Ever continued to feel the emotions long after the conversation has happened? If you have then don't worry, you're not alone, this happens to most of us at some time.

Once a head teacher asked me to train her on successful difficult conversations. She told me she'd had a difficult issue with a lady in her school and that she took this woman on holiday with her; she was by the pool with her, at dinner with her and on the beach with her.

I thought 'Why would you take this person on holiday with you?' and then I realised, she wasn't physically with her, she was in her head throughout the holiday! This head teacher was re-living, re-playing and re-inventing the conversation she'd had and it ruined her summer holiday.

Part of having successful difficult conversations is being able to manage your own emotions during and after and thankfully there is a simple, but highly effective, piece of psychology that will help you with this.

The theory behind the skills

Eric Berne gave us *Transactional Analysis* (TA) in the '60s, which has evolved and developed in the years since and provides a useful framework for understanding all human interactions.

It's wonderfully simple; in fact the hardest thing about it is the name! It proposes that people move between three broad roles:

Parent (P)
Adult (A)
Child (C)

Both Parent and Child have several modes within them and we will look at each in turn.

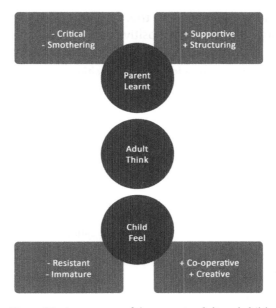

Figure 17: A summary of the parent, adult and child
in transactional analysis

Parent

The Parent ego state of the psyche contains the beliefs, admonitions, feelings and behaviours of parent figures accumulated during our formative years. These are the rules, opinions and actions we absorb and role model growing up. And they stay in the psyche throughout life as the *Critical Parent* and the *Supportive Parent*. When we feel threatened we can become defensive and call on the *Critical Parent* mode to judge, criticise, complain and lecture.

We often hear ourselves sounding just like our mum or dad or other parent figures!

You will see in Figure 18 there are four modes of the Parent ego state, some positive and some negative

Negative parent roles	Positive parent roles
The critical parent	*The supportive parent*
Judgemental Authoritative Telling others off Patronising Knows best	Caring Nurturing Considerate
The smothering parent	*The structuring parent*
Over protective Spoiling Interfering Suffocating	Caring but firm Offers constructive criticism Helps to set boundaries Helps to organise

Figure 18: The four versions of the parent role

Child

In Berne's model, the *Adapted Child* ego state is the part of the psyche developed in childhood (and throughout life) to follow the rules in order to get accepted, loved and cared for.

The *positive Adapted Child (AC)* is co-operative and compliant while the negative AC can be rebellious and resistant. The TA model has been further developed to recognise a creative child, with positive traits such as being creative, fun-loving and spontaneous and negative aspects such as being wild and irresponsible, in the immature child. The Child part of the psyche stays with us throughout life and we can easily regress into this state in certain situations and relationships.

As we grow up we can still show childlike behaviours.

I'm sure we've all wished another adult would 'grow up' and at times we see ourselves behaving in childlike ways. This ego state can be driven by strong emotions.

Negative child roles	Positive child roles
Resistant	*Co-operative*
Oppositional	Seeks to please
Stubborn	Wants to help
Obstinate	Wants validation
Immature	*Creative*
Doesn't take responsibility	Fun
See things as 'not fair'	Spontaneous
Can be reckless	Likes to play
Impulsive	Energetic

Figure 19: The four versions of the child role

Adult

Adult is an ego state which functions in the here and now with rational thinking, emotions and behaviour. In this state we are in control of our feelings and aware when feelings are not backed by evidence. I'm sure you have relationships that are *Adult* in this way with people you go to for the best advice and clarity. These people help you see things clearly and untangle your thinking.

The *Adult* ego state is evidence based, rational, not threatening or threatened. It uses:

- *Open questions*
- *Comparative expressions*
- *Reasoned statements*

- *True, false, probably, possibly, I think, I realise, I see, I believe, in my opinion*
- *Objective understanding of reality*

For difficult conversations we want to be functioning in the *Adult* state.

Being the adult

The benefit of being an adult in difficult conversations is two-fold, firstly the conversation is likely to go better, and secondly you're less likely to mentally chew on the conversation afterwards so it lets you manage emotions before, during and after the conversation. I've certainly never enjoyed reliving difficult conversations in my head and going through all the associated emotions. It's not physically or mentally healthy and I'm sure we all have better things to do with our evenings!

So how do you get to be *Adult* when you need it most? As I'm sure you've gathered from the nature of this book this is a skill that requires practice.

Even the most Adult people I know sometimes get triggered into an unhelpful *Parent* or *Child* state in situations that require a difficult conversation. So don't give yourself a hard time if you don't always remain *Adult* in these situations as they are useful to learn from.

Explaining and training on how to be in the adult role is another whole book but some quick tips you can use are:

1. Being Adult is like being a scientist – look for evidence.

2. Staying in Adult means making sure our emotions don't get the better of us. If you're feeling emotional in a situation you might find sharing that emotion useful.

3. Deep breathing is a key technique because when we're stressed or anxious our breathing tends to become faster and shallower. Before heading into a difficult conversation take three very slow breaths: slow as you breathe in and slow as you breathe out. Give your brain the oxygen it needs.

ACTIVITY

If you find you're struggling being in the Adult state try thinking through these questions:

*   *Who am I most Adult with? What would I say to this person?*
*   *What would I think and feel in my Adult state?*
*   *What would I do if functioning in Adult?*
*   *How would I sit?*
*   *How would I sound?*

I find being aware of *Transactional Analysis* and the games and roles we play goes a long way in helping people be more *Adult*. The fact is we are grown-up in many situations; we just sometimes get triggered and pulled off course in difficult conversations.

Part 3: STORM structure for the conversation

The third element needed to master a successful difficult conversation is structure. I use a simple five-part system for difficult conversations using the acronym STORM, which reminds us of Tuckman's Group Formation and the importance of *storming*:

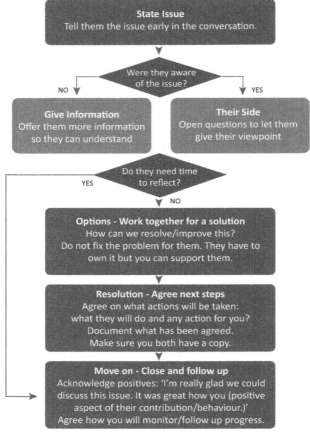

State Issue
Tell them the issue early in the conversation.

Were they aware of the issue?

NO

YES

Give Information
Offer them more information so they can understand

Their Side
Open questions to let them give their viewpoint

Do they need time to reflect?

YES

NO

Options - Work together for a solution
How can we resolve/improve this?
Do not fix the problem for them. They have to own it but you can support them.

Resolution - Agree next steps
Agree on what actions will be taken:
what they will do and any action for you?
Document what has been agreed.
Make sure you both have a copy.

Move on - Close and follow up
Acknowledge positives: 'I'm really glad we could discuss this issue. It was great how you (positive aspect of their contribution/behaviour.)'
Agree how you will monitor/follow up progress.

Figure 20: STORM flowchart© to structure
your difficult conversation

In summary the STORM structure is:

- **State the issue** – tell them what the issue is and what outcome would you like from the conversation
- **Their side** – find out what they think
- **Options** – work together to find ways to resolve or at least move the issue forward
- **Resolution** - agree on what actions will be taken
- **Move on** – clarify what has been agreed

CHAPTER SUMMARY

- *High performing teams are really good at dealing with conflict*
- *All teams go through a process of 'storming' and this is the most important stage of team development*
- *To have a successful difficult conversation you need: trust, emotional management and structure*

Chapter 7
Great leaders grow their good people

'The best way to find yourself is to lose yourself in the service of others.'
Mahatma Gandhi

In this chapter:
- *How to know what approach to use to get the best from others*
- *A look at strengths-based development*
- *Creating a coaching environment; and*
- *The power of celebration in reinforcing the culture you want*

GREAT LEADERS GROW THEIR GOOD PEOPLE

Great leaders are very focused on people. They want the right people on their team and they want them to grow and keep on growing. **Essentially great leaders develop their team the way a great teacher develops children in class.**

People are almost always the biggest cost in an organisation and they are absolutely the greatest asset. Great leaders grow their good people to outstanding and they grow their top talent to dazzling excellence. But developing highly talented people can be daunting because it's far easier to mentor someone who doesn't have your skills and knowledge than to stretch to develop someone who is more skilled or knowledgeable than you! What could I have taught Einstein about physics? He knows far more than I do, but teaching children about physics is easier, because I know more than they do.

Great leaders know their whole team needs developing and they make sure all, including their top talent, are grown by creating opportunities, providing internal and external support for them and providing resources. Several of the traits of a 'transformational leader' do exactly that:

1. They challenge their team to be creative, to push the boundaries of how they would normally work and the provide intellectual stimulation
2. They are very focused on the individual; everyone can approach the leader with ideas and the leader supports and encourages team members

I've seen the harsh reality of what happens when great teachers are not grown.

I was coaching a teacher who was extraordinary: every lesson was a work of art and she still wanted to do better. It wasn't enough that every observation she'd ever had had been rated outstanding, she was driven to do her best for the children she taught and that meant continually improving her teaching. She was a real team player as well; always looking for ways to improve the way her year group worked. Wouldn't we all love to have more teachers like her in our schools? But she was seriously thinking about leaving teaching.

She had lost her excitement for it and didn't know how to improve further despite feeling she could. It was almost as if being outstanding was no longer a medal but more like a millstone around her neck.

Thankfully she attended some training that taught her a range of innovative techniques for the classroom and she became energised to try them for the benefit of her children's learning.

This experience also unlocked what she needed to do to keep herself engaged and inspired; she needed to keep learning how to improve her practice. She needed to be pro-active in seeking out training opportunities. Advanced training did exist but it was harder to find because she was already functioning at an outstanding level. If she'd not found this then the teaching profession would have lost a valuable asset; a superb teacher committed to teaching inspiring lessons every day.

PEOPLE ARE YOUR KEY DRIVER TO SUCCESS

I've noticed in schools, and most organisations, that the opportunity to grow their staff further isn't capitalised on. This is really important if you want a high performing team, essential in delivering exceptional education and creating the your dream school.

There are many ways to develop your team and I think these work well in schools:

1. Flexing your leadership style
2. Growing strengths
3. Creating a great coaching environment
4. Celebrating with your team

FLEXING YOUR LEADERSHIP STYLE

The competency curve

This is a really useful tool in understanding where people currently sit and what they need from their leader.

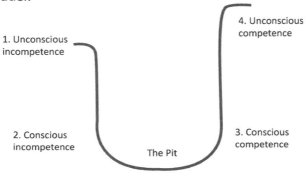

Figure 21: The competency curve

Let me explain how this lop-sided curve works in the learning journey.

1.   At the beginning of learning a new skill we are *unconsciously incompetent:* you don't know what you don't know. Let's say you are learning to drive a car, you think 'Driving is easy, everyone is doing it; it's just about steering the car and changing gears. I'm going to get this in no time!' You are in a state that you might call ignorant bliss; you're unaware (unconscious) of how hard the task will be because you don't yet know how to do it (incompetent).

2.   You then move to *conscious incompetence:* you now know (conscious) that you don't have this skill (incompetence); you know you don't know how to drive. There seems to be so much to think about, mirrors, indicators, clutch, brake and accelerator.

This stage can feel quite overwhelming and leave people wondering if they'll ever master the skill, or even get good enough to get behind the wheel. This is 'the pit'.

3.   Next is *conscious competence:* here you know what you know. You know how to drive (competence) but you have to think about it (conscious). So you get in the car, seat belt on, mirror, handbrake, clutch, you go through the steps and drive well but you are thinking about what you are doing so if the passenger starts talking to you, you probably can't hold a proper conversation because you need to concentrate.

4.   Finally we move to *unconscious competence:* you don't know (unconscious) what you know (competence) and this is the stage of the experienced driver. Tell me: when you drive, do you think about it? I doubt it; you're probably thinking about your day, picking up the shopping, collecting the kids, what you're doing tonight or plans for the weekend. What you're not doing is consciously thinking about driving and that is because you are now so competent at the multi-faceted process you can do it unconsciously.

This same journey is experienced when people take on a new job or responsibility:

•   *Stage 1 Unconscious Incompetence:* 'It's pretty straight-forward to be a deputy head, I can do that.'

•   *Stage 2 Conscious Incompetence:* ' I've got to present to the Governors? I need to get better at managing stakeholders? I need to deal with child protection? This is hard; I don't know how to do these things.'

•   *Stage 3 Conscious Competence:* 'Okay, I've made my own checklist for Governor meetings and scheduled a meeting to run through my preparation with my Head, which will give me time to make an amendments.'

- *Stage 4 Unconscious Competence:* 'The new Assistant Head thought I ran the Governor meeting really well. I hadn't really planned it but I guess I did!'

I see light bulbs go on over school leaders' heads when I share this model because often there is at least one person in the team who is, or has recently, gone through this process and recognises when they were in that difficult 'pit'.

Competency curves build on each other and that's why it's higher on one side because when you move through the stages you have more skills when you reach the other side. We move to a new competency curve usually because we are at the top of a previous competency curve when we are competent. And so it's not surprising that feeling incompetent can come as quite a surprise as we embark on a new curve.

Understanding that the curve is a normal part of the learning process helps people see how they are progressing.

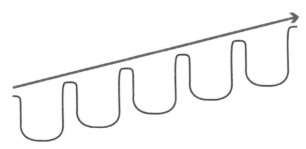

Figure 22: The upward trend of competency curves

Moving to new competency curves happens for any skills development, be that a promotion or a within role development; for example an advanced teacher will go through various competency curves as they improve their range of skills.

Four leadership styles to support the competency curve

In growing your team, each staff member will move through competency curves. Part of your skill as Head will be to know where they are and what they need from you.

Mentor	Delegate
Unconscious incompetence	Unconscious competence
(Don't know what you don't know)	(Don't know what you know)
Direct	Coach
Conscious incompetence	Conscious competence
(Know what you don't know)	(Know what you know)

Figure 23: The best leadership style to use according to where someone is on the competency curve

It's really important to focus on the specific task or skills someone is working on, for example you might have a wonderfully competent teacher leading literacy, who is struggling to get the team on board with his ideas. The skill that needs developing is team engagement and buy-in, not his skill with teaching literacy.

When to mentor

When someone is in Stage 1 of the competency curve they don't know what they don't know and so your role is to mentor them. This means you will give them both the benefit of your experience and knowledge and help them generate their own answers and insights through coaching style questions. Mentoring is really a blend of instructing someone and coaching them.

When to direct

In Stage 2, when someone knows they don't know, they need you to be directive and tell them what to do. Have you ever had a time when you were floundering and not had a clue what to do and someone has come along and given you clear directions? You probably felt relieved that some-one helped you in such an authoritative way. 'Telling people what to do' has got a bad reputation but there's a time and place for it. I was training a school leader-ship team on 'Flexing your leadership style' and a team member shared how he had been in this helpless place, and how he and his Head had muddled through but reflecting on the experience, he realised he needed someone to tell him what to do in a straight-forward way.

When to coach

In stage 3, when someone knows what they know, we tend to use coaching. Coaching has been over-used and generalised, almost as if it is the only method, which isn't correct in my opinion and experience.

Coaching does work pretty well across all of these stages, better in some than others, but it's not the best approach in every situation. In stage 3 we often find staff have good skills but are de-motivated, bored or frustrated, so coaching is a good approach because it can unlock the person.

Not everyone who has coaching is de-motivated; in fact often they are quite the opposite because coaching works well in developing highly competent and motivated people as well. When I coach Heads they are usually already outstanding or strive to be and they are very motivated.

When to delegate

Stage 4, where people are unconsciously competent, requires the leader to delegate tasks to them and also offer coaching support. Now a few words of advice about true delegation because I see a lot of 'glorified delegation', which is not really delegation. 'Glorified delegation' is when you give a staff member a list of things to do for you in the same way you might instruct a secretary or personal assistant.

True delegation means giving an accurate description of the result required and letting the person come up with the plan of how to achieve it. They might even generate a vision of where they will take it and how to get there. We give them as many of their requested resources as possible and let them update us while giving them control and responsibility.

So if you wanted to delegate improving writing across the school you might say to your carefully chosen team member who is unconsciously competent in the relevant skills:

'I would love it if you took the lead in improving writing across the school. All I know is I want our children to all hit national standards by Year 6 and for those who have special needs I want them to show excellent progress.

For me it's really important that our children go to secondary school with a really good writing level, it's not just about hitting the target grade it's really about them being able to produce quality writing. At the moment I don't believe we are achieving this across the school. I'd really like you to lead this and to come up with a plan to make this a reality, what do you think?'

In this example the target is given (national standards by Year 6 and children producing quality writing), but if you wanted them to take the lead on the whole piece, including the target you might say:

'I would love it if you took the lead in improving writing across the school. For me it's really important that our children go to secondary school with a really good writing level and writing ability so they get off to a flying start and at the moment I don't believe we are achieving this. I'd really like you to lead this, for you to decide what our goal or vision is and come up with a plan to make this a reality, what do you think?'

That is true delegation. Expect lots of enthusiastic questions from this person, who will be motivated to take on the challenge.

ACTIVITY

Select some people in your school and work out what leadership approach they need to develop further.

GROWING STRENGTHS

Does everyone in your team know their own and everyone else's strengths? Chances are people know what people are 'good at', but that's not necessarily their real strengths.

The difference between strengths and competence

A strength is something you are naturally adept at and by investing time to develop this skill you can expect to become extremely capable. This is very clear in the sporting world. Andy Murray was naturally good at tennis and with countless hours of training has become world class.

Likewise Sir Chris Hoy became a champion cyclist and Lewis Hamilton a champion at Formula One racing.

In business Sir Richard Branson was naturally talented at business from a young age and spent many years working at business to become a global entrepreneur. Their secret to success is focusing on their strengths. I reckon Andy Murray isn't working on his backstroke! A natural strength is usually something we enjoy, which is not surprising, because pleasure comes from a sense of competence and empowerment.

We can be competent at our strengths but we can also be competent at things that are not our strengths.

When I worked in business a colleague was very competent at running disciplinary meetings and reaching a satisfying conclusion. She was so good that the Head Office team would draw on her skills constantly. However she didn't enjoy these meetings. She was good at them because she did so many. And so this was an area of competence but not one of her strengths to enjoy.

Strengths are skills we have a passion and talent for; it's essentially what we are famous for. Some people, like the sports stars I mentioned, discover their strengths early. However it's not always easy to discern our strengths. Everyone has several strengths and there is a major benefit to your team when you identify each person's talents, so they become a 'go to' person for that expertise.

ACTIVITY

What are the skills you are naturally good at and enjoy? Try to come up with five. You might want to ask family, friends and colleagues.

(People often undervalue their own strengths, because they find them so easy. Keep this in mind when asking others because you might discount what they say). How could you grow this strength and become even more brilliant at it?

ACTIVITY

Think about your team, what would you say their individual strengths are? Ask them if they agree.

Work on strengths and areas for development

Focusing on strengths does not mean forgetting about the areas we need to develop (weaknesses). There will be tasks where staff members need a level of competence and must improve, but focusing on strengths is different from the way most of us have been brought up.

Think back to when you were at school, or with your own children, and imagine the following grades in their end of year report:

English = A
Maths = D
History = B

Which subject would you invest in with extra tuition or support? I suspect maths and you wouldn't be alone because this is an important subject and the grade is low so that would make perfect sense. But these grades also show that English is something this child is good at and might even be a strength.

I was working with a leadership team in a school and one teacher was underperforming and although she managed to scrape a 'good' observation, there was enough evidence for the leaders to feel she wasn't performing sufficiently. The Phase Leader had tried diligently to improve the teacher's performance for some time but felt they'd reached the need for formal Capability procedures.

In a coaching session I asked if she could give the struggling teacher any role in the school she would naturally excel at, what would it be? As it turns out she was excellent at languages and this was a skill the school wanted to keep developing. She realised that if the teacher covered planning, preparation and assessment time (PPA) with a language focus this would be a perfect fit for her and the school. The difference in the Phase Leader when she realised this was delightful to witness! She was excited for the teacher and how talented she would be in this new role and how much she would now enjoy teaching. With Capability avoided and a teacher delivering to her strengths, we all celebrated a win-win!

Make it fun and focused

Working on strengths should be fun and enjoyable, but with focus. A way to have all of these elements is for people, once they understand their strengths, to create a vision for themselves. What would they be doing in their role if they were using their strengths? How would this feel for them? What would others say about them? How would they continue to grow their strengths? Create the picture of success they are heading toward and then work on the plan to achieve this.

Another way to make sure strengths development is kept alive is to include it in performance reviews. With my teams I would have four development objectives; two about developing skills and two about developing their strengths.

ACTIVITY

Create a picture of success for your strengths. What would you be doing if you were using your strengths as much as possible? And what impact would this have?

Creating a great coaching environment

Part of growing your team and your talent is to have self-reflective practitioners and coaching is an ideal way of doing this. It gives people the space to examine what they have done and how they want to improve in a way that is best for them.

Coaching is often a misunderstood skill.

As a qualified coach I often hear people claiming they have been 'coaching' someone but I can see they were not coaching in the true sense. I see people coaching with little training in any models or frameworks, without necessary reflective coaching practice for themselves.

To put this into context to gain a Diploma in Coaching you will usually undertake between 40 to 60 hours of training and need to have practised coaching sessions for at least 50 hours, all with self-reflective notes. This usually takes between one and two years to complete. Qualifying with a Diploma in Coaching is a large investment of time and money. However it is possible to create a good coaching culture without this high level of investment using some expert support.

Coaching is not a natural skill for the vast majority of people. Yet because it is essentially a conversation, people often think they are 'coaching' when they are not. So I want to explain what real coaching is and is not.

What coaching is

This is how I explain coaching when I start to coach someone new:

Coaching is about understanding where you want to get to, where you currently are and how you can go from here to there. And don't worry if you're not sure about where you want to get to, I can help you figure that out.

Coaching is about change; it's future-focused and action-based, which means I'm not going to ask you to lie on a couch and tell me about your childhood. You can if you want to and as long as it's relevant to your goals, however if we start to meander, I will steer us back on track.

Coaching is an equal partnership between you and me; my role is to help you find your answers and how to achieve your goal. It is a journey and there can be ups and downs. It's also likely that your thoughts and insights will continue outside of our coaching sessions, which is normal and fine. You are also free to give me feedback because my aim is to coach you as well as I can to help you achieve your goals so any feedback is welcome.

Coaching is confidential, so I won't tell others what you talk to me about; however you are free to talk to whomever you like about the sessions. I might refer to 'a coachee' I've worked with to give an example but I won't identify that person. The only time I would break confidentiality is if you were intending to, or had, broken the law; coaching is not above the law and I am required to report this.

Coaching is non-advisory and judgement-free, which means, by and large, I'm not going to offer you any advice. If I do think there is something that might be useful, be it information or advice, I will share it but if it doesn't work for you we'll just discard it.

In terms of being judgement-free, if you were to tell me you want to earn a million pounds, become an astronaut or be the best teacher in the country, I won't judge you, verbally or non-verbally. I will simply ask questions to help you understand what you need to do to achieve your goal.

What coaching is *not*

Coaching is not:

- Just a chat
- A place to have sympathy, it's a place for empathy
- Telling someone what they should do
- Solving someone's problems or goals for them
- Coaching someone to get to the answer you want them to get to

This last point is particularly important and a common mistake, one I made myself before I completing my coaching diploma. **Coaching isn't a clever way of making someone get to the answer you want by asking questions that lead to the person to a pre-determined conclusion.** That's just manipulative.

I've seen lots of people use coaching in this way and they usually get frustrated because they can't seem to ask the right questions to lead to the answer they want; therein lies the problem. As coaches we don't know the answer, even if we think we do, our job is to help the other person find their own answer.

When to coach

Earlier in this chapter I gave a model for knowing which leadership style to use in which situation and according to that model coaching is best used when you have someone who has a good competence level but low motivation. I have coached a lot of people and I can tell you that not everyone I coach falls into this quadrant. In fact coaching works well for those we would delegate to and even with those we would mentor, which you will remember is a blend of coaching and directing. The one place coaching really doesn't seem to work is when someone needs straight-forward telling what to do.

When I first joined the John Lewis Leadership Programme I had already worked in a few roles since leaving university, and so when I met with the trainer responsible for the graduates she used to coach me and I loved it because I was in the right place to be coached: I had a good level of competence and a good level of motivation and coaching helped drive my performance forward in a way I shaped.

A friend of mine on the scheme was straight out of university and our trainer also coached her; she loathed this, saying to me after meetings 'I don't want to be coached. I just need to be told what I should be doing!'

She was very bright and extremely capable (she is now senior in the business and set to go even further). It was just at that time and place a directive, not coaching, style was what she needed.

Coaching skills

Coaching skills are great skills to have as they make human interactions so much easier. I honestly look back over situations I've been in and wish I had the skills then that I have now because I would have handled them so much better.

You will never go wrong by developing your coaching skills. I have already covered two of them in building rapport and questioning and listening skills.

Other skills in coaching include the use of models such as the GROW model, approaches like cognitive behavioural coaching, Gestalt coaching and person-centred coaching and skills like summarising, clarifying, feedback, reflection, challenging, values work, limiting beliefs - the list goes on.

Fundamentally if you develop the skills of building rapport, questioning and listening and how to use the GROW model you will be in better place than most when you coach. These skills are best developed by layering them on to one another.

The GROW model

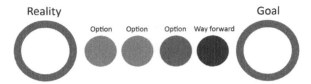

Figure 24: The GROW model of coaching

The GROW model of coaching (Whitmore, 2002) is a very useful starting point because it is an easy way to understand the theory and start to practise coaching. The model structures the conversation like this:

- **Goal** – what does the person want to achieve?
- **Reality** – where are they now?
- **Options** – what could they do to move toward their goal?
- **Way forward** – what will they choose to do?

This is a very brief description of each stage as a memory aid should you want a quick overview of the model, but each step needs some expansion if you want to use the model effectively.

Goal

I usually spend the whole first session working on the person's goal because the more specific it is the more likely they are to achieve it. You want to understand why someone wants to achieve this goal and to help them drill down into what they really want. Some examples of questions you might ask are:

- What do you want to achieve?
- How will you know you have achieved this?
- What will this give you?

You then want to get to the point where the coachee creates a SMARTER goal, which is:

- **S**pecific – if the goal is specific enough you will both have the same picture of success for it.
- **M**easurable – how will the coachee know when they have achieved this?
- **A**chievable – does the coachee think it is achievable, even if it's challenging?
- **R**ealistic – this should be based on the understanding of where the coachee is and what they can expect.
- **T**ime – when will the goal be achieved? Be really specific about this and get a date and time agreed.
- **E**xciting – what excites the coachee about this goal?
- **R**elevant – how does this fit into the bigger picture of the coachee's life?

Once you have the goal you should both write it down. It's really important for the coachee to write down the goal in their words, because there is a power and commitment that often comes with the act of writing; it's like pinning their colours to the mast.

Reality

Here you want to understand and explore what is currently going on for the person. Some of the reality of the situation will inevitably come out while you explore the goal and that's fine. Be careful not to treat this as a fact-finding stage so you can present them with the solution. They will come up with their own solution. Questions you might ask during this stage are:

- What is currently happening for you with this?
- Where are you with this goal at the moment?
- What makes this a challenge?

Once we have a clear goal and have explored the current situation we can move into finding possible ways to move toward the goal.

Options

During this stage of the model you want the coachee to brainstorm as many ideas as they can to move them toward their goal. It's important to focus on possibilities and not worry about whether they are realistic because you want their creative juices to flow. Usually people come up with the obvious ideas first and you can tell by their unenthusiastic body language they don't really like them. Questions to help them come up with more ideas are:

- What could you do to achieve your goal?
- What would someone else advise you to do?
- What would an expert say?

Really push your coachee, in a supportive way, to go beyond the obvious, top of mind ideas because then the best brainwaves come up!

Way forward

This is where you ask your coachee which of their ideas they are going to take action on. They might pick one or they might pick a few. For each idea they need to commit to what they are going to do and by when. Ascertain how committed they are to the action. Questions you might ask are:

- Which options are you most drawn to?
- Which ones don't you like and want to rule out?
- On a scale of 1 - 10 how committed are you to taking each action?

At your next coaching meeting you would start by revisiting the actions they have taken, how they got on with them and check the goal is still what they want to be working on; if it's not they can change it.

There is a lot more to coaching than I have explained here and a multitude of books and courses on the subject.

The GROW model was created by John Whitmore, one of the 'fathers of coaching', and his book 'Coaching for Performance' (Whitmore, Coaching For Performance: Growing People, Performance and Purpose, 2002) is a perfect place to learn more about this model if you want to.

CELEBRATE WITH YOUR TEAM
AND REINFORCE THE CULTURE

Children grow when we focus on what they do well and support them in their learning. As a teacher you would have found many ways throughout the day to praise and celebrate the children in your class. The same applies with adults. You might not do it to the same extent, but you will need to praise regularly to reinforce your culture.

Every school is different and you will know how best to pitch this in your school. **In one Midlands school, the Head wouldn't praise teachers in front of other teachers because culturally this would lead to resentment. While this was not ideal, the Head was working on ways to praise and celebrate his team's successes.**

Celebration builds momentum as long as it's genuine. It is really a form of feedback and needs to be specific in stating what's being celebrated.

Celebrate with the whole team,
mini-teams and individuals

There are points in the year which allow you to celebrate as a whole team, some will appear like a 'good' Ofsted judgement or getting your best end of year results, and some will be part of the school calendar, like Christmas, the end of term and the end of year.

It might also be that a year group has done particularly well in developing their children, it might be a subject co-ordinator has driven their subject forward and really made a positive impact; it might be a teaching assistant has become a higher level teaching assistant; it might be the site manager oversaw an overhaul to the heating system without any disruption to the school.

It's worth taking some time to plan what and when you will be celebrating as well as being tuned into the opportunities that present themselves day to day. You might also want to create some new celebrations, such as Teacher of the Year or Mid-day Supervisor of the Term awards.

The best advice I can give is think like you did when you were a class teacher. How you can apply some of those same techniques to celebrate with your team and highlight the behaviours and performance levels you want across your school?

With teams and individuals you will have a feeling about the right way to celebrate or reward them.

With teams and individuals you will have a feeling about the right way to celebrate or reward them.

When I was finance manager at Peter Jones I wanted to acknowledge and reward the work of one of my team members. He worked in finance and was brilliant at making sure money wasn't going to waste so a monetary reward seemed like the wrong thing to do, instead I gave him an extra day's leave, which he was delighted with.

Celebrations can be low cost; certificates and thoughtful thank you cards go a long way as do boxes of chocolates and bunches of flowers, whatever is right for the individual.

The best part about celebrating success is that it feels good for you and those who are celebrating and, if your school culture is good, individual celebrations will feel enjoyable for the whole team as well.

CHAPTER SUMMARY

- *Focus on growing your team's ability to do their job exceptionally well*
- *Try to adapt your leadership style to meet the needs of your team*
- *Celebrate your team and individuals*

Section 3
Making your dream school a reality

Chapter 8
Getting past the obstacles

'Success consists of going from failure to failure
without loss of enthusiasm.'
Winston Churchill

In this chapter:
- *Four common obstacles which could get in your way*
- *How to overcome them and create your dream school*

Creating a culture of excellence is hard, but most challenges are made easier when we have some guidance and I hope this book has been able to help you navigate the way. But just as going on a journey is easier with a map it doesn't mean the terrain won't be tricky in places. Often anything worth fighting for takes a healthy dose of determination.

Expect obstacles, they are a natural and essential part of this journey, as are setbacks and backtracking at times. I'm sure you didn't get to where you are without overcoming many challenges and the same tenacity is required as you go forward. As they say, **successful people just make their mistakes faster.**

I often get coaching clients to consider what obstacles could get in their way to achieving their goal so they can be prepared to deal with them and stay on track. If you visualise and collect the possible setbacks and obstacles you could come across on your path then you will see patterns emerge. This provides useful insight about the root cause.

There are four common obstacles I see in creating the best school culture:

1. Time
2. Mindset
3. Knowledge and skills
4. Fear of success

OBSTACLE 1: I DON'T HAVE ENOUGH TIME!

Who does? We all have the same amount of hours in our day; it's just how we use our time that makes the difference. When I see outstanding Heads in schools with tough demographics or a low budget or any number of other 'reasons' they might not be outstanding, I see they prioritise: they focus relentlessly on what they believe will make the difference and keep working on these areas.

No-one wants to be a busy fool

Many people don't like change but we often hear the mantra that change is good. Or is change bad? It depends. Changing direction constantly is often not good. But it happens when a school is unclear about where it's going and why, without a clear vision and plan.

At its worst erratic change looks like this: a new idea comes in, we run after it, train it, talk about it, and make sure people are using it but then we don't seem to get results. But thankfully another new idea has come along and this one really works!

Now we run after that, train it, talk about it and make sure people are using it and there might be some results, but again not the big impact we hoped for. But wait! Here's another great idea! And this cycle can go on, sometimes getting results, sometimes not. This type of knee-jerk change can be detrimental and a waste of time.

Schools rated *Special Measures* or *Requires Improvement* require rapid change strategies while in *Good* and *Outstanding* schools a lower level of targeted change is required.

Make time count by focusing on
what makes a difference

In thriving cultures there is a clear direction and understanding of galvanising their valuable resources to achieve their vision and stay focused. So if a school wants to deliver the best education they know that exceptional teaching is the key. Therefore teachers and teaching assistants are their most precious resource. The school then does everything possible to support the teaching staff.

Use your time wisely,
it's the most precious resource you have

How you use your time will be a big factor in how well your school is led. I'm not saying work more hours. Every Head I know already works too many hours as it is. I'm saying use your time to best effect. That might even mean taking time out, away from school once a month, so you can stop and think without distractions. How often do you get to really think and plan about your school?

We can often get locked into mundane daily tasks. When we get resourceful we discover ways to remove or at least reduce these time consuming habits. And we resist getting seduced by activities we enjoy but add no value. This means we free ourselves up to find ways to reach our goals.

ACTIVITY

Write down activities you could stop doing or delegate that would give you more time to focus on activities that will make a positive difference to your school?

Be strategic in your own use of you, after all you are the key to creating the school you have always dreamt of leading.

OBSTACLE 2: MINDSET

Your mind set and that of your team will affect how likely you are to bring your dream school into reality and this can be broken down into two main areas: responsibility and waiting for perfection.

Responsibility

At the start of the summer holidays I was having lunch with a head teacher (also a friend) and she was telling me how her leadership team was not happy with the performance of some of the Newly Qualified Teachers. She listened to their grievances and asked what her leaders were doing to improve them. Her question was met with silence. The performance of new teachers is really the responsibility of their leadership; their job is to develop them by imparting knowledge and skills. Simply complaining that new teachers are not good enough is a cop out.

I'm afraid to say that I do hear leaders complain about how they've 'not got a strong enough teacher' or how 'the assistant head isn't capable enough' and so on.

A leader's job is to take responsibility for the people they serve. If staff fail it's our fault as leaders; if they succeed it's their success. That is my view on leadership, it's not shared by everyone, but it's a guiding principle that has served me well. In the same way we looked at the possible 'reasons' or excuses for not being outstanding, we need to ensure we are taking full responsibility for our people and lead them to success whenever possible.

Waiting for perfection

When we have a full set of teaching assistants'; 'When people stop leaving'; 'When we have better end of year results'…there is always a reason to postpone focusing on creating your high performing culture.

Outstanding Heads have rarely, if ever, been in the perfect conditions to create an outstanding school, so you don't need to wait either. There might some very good reasons for you to wait, but make sure they are really good reasons. Perfection doesn't happen often, and you and I only have our lifetimes, so let's be aware of the danger in waiting for all the right conditions and just crack on anyway!

ACTIVITY

Write down any mindset barriers you or your team might have. These are limiting thoughts that might be inadvertently holding you back.

OBSTACLE 3: KNOWLEDGE AND SKILLS

The third obstacle is making the time and effort to gain the knowledge and skills you need.

If you always do what you've always done you'll always get what you got

Leadership skills take practice and time. We will get some things wrong and we will keep trying to get it right, like when we learn a new sport or musical instrument. But as leaders we will all keep learning new skills so we can keep leading at a higher level than before. I love the saying 'if you always do what you've always done you'll always get what you always got'!

This is a really useful reminder of the fact **if we want a different result we need to do something differently.** Another favourite of mine is the 'definition of insanity: doing the same thing and expecting a different result'. Are you adept at those three core leadership skills? Is there any additional knowledge you want to gain?

Because we're leaders doesn't mean we have to get everything right all of the time, although I know it often feels this way! If you're worried about making mistakes or what your team will think of you then share with them that you are striving to develop your leadership. After all you probably know how they are all developing in their roles and it makes you more authentic if you share what you are grappling with. Sometimes staff can forget that even though you are the head teacher you're human as well!

ACTIVITY

So what skills or knowledge do you need to develop or gain to create the school you've always wanted to lead?

OBSTACLE 4: DON'T BE AFRAID OF SUCCESS

You might be surprised that some people can be afraid of success. We usually think of success as a something positive but it scares some people. **I've heard a lot of Heads say 'The problem is once I get to outstanding I have to stay there!'** They view the success of achieving a rating of *outstanding* as presenting its own problem.

And they would be right to be concerned if they have created an outstanding school in the wrong way: where they are the sole person keeping up standards by micro-managing every facet of the school. You see a really great school, one with a high performance culture, should be outstanding even if you, the Head, went away for a term or two.

With a high performing culture the hard work is in getting there; staying there should be far easier. **By creating this culture your team will be pursuing excellence, which should take your school beyond outstanding.**

CHAPTER SUMMARY

- *Use your time wisely*
- *Be proactive in improving your use of time*
- *Be aware of how your own mind set might get in your way, including a fear of success*

Chapter 9
You and your leaders must lead change

'It is no use walking anywhere to preach
unless our walking is our preaching.'
Francis of Assisi

In this chapter:
* *Making sure you develop yourself and your leaders*
* *Making sure you are supported*
* *Choosing the best support*

To create the school you have always dreamt of leading you are going to be the one at the forefront of this change, followed closely by your senior and middle leaders.

WHAT DO YOU NEED?

Your continuing professional development

Most Heads I know focus on their own continuing professional development (CPD) last, if ever, but if you're to lead this change you will need to think about yourself. Often when a Head asks me for coaching they often say they've decided to invest in themselves for the first time in years. **Developing yourself is not selfish or self-centred; it's necessary.** So what's on your CPD plan that will make a big difference to your leadership style and job fulfilment?

DON'T DO IT ON YOUR OWN

No-one is an island and you certainly have enough on your shoulders before developing your own skills further, so get help in the form that works best for you. That might be training courses, shadowing other Heads, finding a mentor or coach, it might be regular feedback from your senior leaders or others – choose whatever will work best for you.

WHAT DO YOUR SENIOR LEADERS NEED?

Much like your own development, what do your senior leaders need in order for them to lead better?

I find that senior leaders usually have the technical knowledge to make them competent in their role, but often need stronger leadership skills to create the dream school. Do they know your expectations really clearly? Are they confident at tackling under-performance or poor adult behaviour? What additional responsibilities could they take on? Are they running performance management or pupil progress meetings? Are they familiar with systems management and using it?

The list of questions could go on but you get the idea! And you know the right questions to ask for your school.

WHAT DO YOUR MIDDLE LEADERS NEED?

You and I know that these guys and gals have a pretty tough job sitting between a rock and hard place: they have the responsibility of leadership but without the authority and they are usually leading their peers. This is one of the hardest positions to be in as a leader. What do you want from your middle leaders? What do they need to meet the expectations for their role? I have often found that middle leader roles are not clearly defined. And middle leaders are often expected to take on roles they haven't been trained in. Make sure they know what is expected and that training is in place to enable them to perform their roles confidently.

I remember a head teacher who wanted to develop his middle leaders who were all responsible for a year group. As we were shaping the programme I asked if they ran the performance management meetings. He said they didn't and that perhaps this was something he needed to let go of and wasn't. 'Maybe...' I said. 'Do they have the skills and knowledge to take this on?' He paused and said they didn't. Therefore we planned to train them up so they could take on this responsibility confidently.

ACTIVITY

Write down what support will enable each of these groups to lead better:
1. *You*
2. *Your senior leaders*
3. *Your middle leaders*

IN-HOUSE VS EXTERNAL TRAINING

Some training will be best delivered by you or by members of your team. I am a fan of in-house training because it's an ideal, and cost effective, way to develop your team and it works well as long as you or someone in your team has the skills and knowledge to share and the time to share it. If you don't then you will probably benefit from external support from experts from other schools or your local authority, online resources, training or consultants.

CHOOSING THE BEST EXTERNAL SUPPORT FOR YOUR SCHOOL

You're going to spend some of your school budget developing your team and they will spend valuable time engaging in that CPD so naturally you will want to get it right. However there are quite a few variables that can stop you from choosing the best solution. I see a lot of variation in how CPD providers are chosen so it's useful to share some common mistakes, which you and your team can avoid when finding suitable support.

1. Clarity – Not being clear about what you want the training to achieve

The most important aspect of making the decision about training is **to work out what you want to be different as a result of the training and how you will know when that has happened.**

When I decided I wanted to train to be a coach I interviewed three training providers because I didn't just want my diploma, I wanted to have the strong foundations to be a capable coach and keep on improving. The training provider I chose needed to care about my coaching skills and want their coaches to be brilliant! They needed to offer ongoing support. With this focus I was able to choose a provider that gave me the best start on my coaching journey and to this day supports my coaching development. Had I gone with the quickest training course I might have acquired my diploma but I'm certain I would not have been as good a coach when I first qualified.

2. Cost – Choosing the cheapest

I know you have budget constraints, this is a reality, and I know this can lead to you choosing a cheaper CPD option. However this can be a false economy because you initially pay less but don't get the result you wanted, which actually means it was a waste of money. I'm not saying you always have to pay top price but be aware when cost is a driving factor and question yourself:

- Can you spend less and really achieve your aim?
- Would it be better to wait until the next financial year and buy the better CPD solution?
- Is it better to not bother with training at all if you can't do it properly and spend the money somewhere else where it will make a greater difference?

3. Time – Going for the quick option

Please don't underestimate how long it can take for us to really learn a new skill or embed and use new knowledge. If you want long lasting change you're unlikely to get that from a one-off training course in a few hours.

I once had a head teacher ask me to teach her team how to have successful difficult conversations in two hours. I told her I could give them some useful overview information but there was no way I could deliver the outcome she wanted in that timeframe! Conversely I worked with a Head who wanted to develop his teachers to an outstanding level and he understood that this work would take a few years to really embed. The goal would need a combination of training and time to put it into action, review and adjust. The last thing he was looking for was a quick fix; he wanted his outcome: consistently outstanding teachers and was willing to put in the effort and resources to make that happen.

I'm not saying a quick option isn't a good one; it can be. But be aware if you're trying to rush something through just to get the job done. You might not get the result you hoped for.

4. Quality – Not checking how effective the training is quantitatively and qualitatively

You will naturally want to check the quality of the CPD you're about to invest in and there are a number of ways to do this. Quantitative methods include tangible results achieved, feedback scores and how many people have been on the training and recommend it.

Qualitative methods are also important because a lot of results from training are not measurable (like increased confidence, clarity or new techniques). And yet these intangibles are so often the reasons for the training. Speak to some of the training provider's clients about the training you are considering. In my experience Heads are very honest with each other about the training they've received and the impact it made.

5. Format – Choosing the wrong training format

'Format' is all about the way training is delivered. Online training might be effective, so might a conference, a course, reading a book or INSET training. **We often accept the training on offer without specifying the format of training to best support the outcome.** This mistake is often made due to cost or time pressures.

For example, imagine you are a class teacher again and you could go on a course about how to be an outstanding teacher. There are courses out there that would help you achieve this aim. But what if you had a programme where someone observed you and gave you feedback or coaching on how to become outstanding where the coach reviewed plans with you to make sure an increasing number of lessons were outstanding and they might team teach or model techniques for you. The latter is more likely to be based in school, very hands on and practical – it also means that the knowledge and skills developed are more likely to be implemented.

The format of the training would help the training be applied and achieve the outcome you're looking for.

We see parallels in the classroom. If we want children to learn about filtering we could simply tell them about the concept but most teachers would use a practical activity because this would lead to better learning. Choose the best method of learning for the learning goal you want to achieve just like a class teacher considers their approach to each lesson to maximise learning and deliver quality first time teaching.

6. Continued support -
Not expecting follow up support

We don't teach children something once, we teach it several times, in different ways, building additional skills as we do and we keep supporting them because we know learning is not a linear, one-off process.

When we, as adults, are being trained, we usually need some ongoing support, so what does the training provide if you need some help a bit further down the line? This might be as simple as a phone call to check how you are getting on or it might be a follow-up session.

I often call school leaders a few weeks after they've had our *Successful Difficult Conversations* training to find out if they had their conversation and how it went. I want the training to have made a positive difference to the problem. A follow-up call is also an opportunity to provide more tips to build their skills.

I believe that for training to be really effective we need some form of ongoing support because just attending a course often isn't enough – it's how you take it forward after the course that really makes the difference.

These mistakes can be summarised by answering the question **'Who or what is going to give you the result you want?'**, if you can answer that question then the chances are you will choose a good training solution.

CHAPTER SUMMARY

- *Make sure you focus on your own development*
- *Invest in your senior leaders*
- *Develop your middle leaders (theirs is a tough job)*
- *Internal CPD is great as long as you have someone with the skills, knowledge and time to deliver it*
- *Be aware of common mistakes people make when choosing external CPD*

Chapter 10

Creating an outstanding school culture

'Only those who will risk going too far can possibly find out how far one can go.'
T. S. Eliot

In this chapter:
- *Culture takes time*
- *Culture is about consistency*
- *Some tips for going the distance*

Creating a compelling vision, making it a reality through good planning, improving performance and behaviour among your team and growing them to perform even better is a lot of work.

SUCCESS HAPPENS OVER TIME

Creating the best school requires the three leadership strategies to be applied consistently well over a period of time.

'One Hit Wonders' on performance or vision or short lived coaching programmes are not likely, on their own, to create the school you want to lead.

Much in the same way classroom management is formed over time and then maintained, cultural change takes years and can easily be undone. That's why when creating a culture the most important tool you have is consistency.

CREATING THE CULTURE OF THE SCHOOL YOU WANT TO LEAD TAKES CONSISTENCY OVER TIME

Consistency doesn't mean a lack of innovation or creativity, if a creative culture is what you have created then consistency will mean you are consistently creative; but knowing the core values of your culture and protecting this ideal culture is important.

Culture is about the right behaviours repeated over time. The consistency of your approach to your team's behaviour will build your culture and if your behaviour is one that resolves poor adult behaviour and under-performance quickly and grows your team to deliver fantastic education then you can begin to imagine the kind of high performing culture you will have nurtured. This will take at least a few years to create and embed even if you excel at the process.

But consistency is hard and can get boring and in my view this is why culture is hard to maintain. For example maintaining focus on your vision can be hard as can implementing your plan; there will be tempting new ideas and tantalising new directions that come along to drag you off track. I'm not saying you won't change your vision but be cautious. If you do revise your vision make sure this is what you really want, not what you think you should want.

KEEPING ON TRACK

With a long journey, like cultural change, it can be easy to forget how far you've come and wander off track. To avoid this you need to keep checking you're on the right path. Here are a few ways you can.

Your strategic triangle is working document

Your strategic triangle is a great tool to keep you forging forward on the right track. Your vision and mission set out where you want to be, but because they will usually be years in the making you need to have some milestones along the way. This is where your strategy, objectives and tactics come into their own. Your key strategic areas will usually change on an annual basis, objectives on a termly basis and your tactics need to be assessed every term. Using your plan as a working document and constantly checking back to see how you are getting on with these will help you assess your progress. I recommend checking and reviewing progress at least once a term and putting that review in the diary for a leadership team meeting.

Decide your mission success criteria

This is an accurate barometer for checking your progress towards your mission and making sure your plan is working. Take your mission and create 'success criteria'. These are the tangible things that will tell you you're achieving your mission and they all need to be things you can tick off.

One school I worked with had a thorough *Success Criteria* that included being the first choice in parents' school selection, real estate agents promoting the school's catchment area along with end of year results. Tick all criteria you are currently meeting and predict when you will achieve the others. These dates should be supported by your strategic plan. On a term or bi-annual basis review the attributes you can tick off and check that actions on your plan are moving you towards the other criteria.

Strategic stepping stones

Another way to keep on track is to create four pictures of progress; this adds a valuable layer of depth and clarity to your strategic plan. You know where you are now, you know where you want to get to and you can create some markers to track progress.

Pick three to five dates on your journey when you believe you would see progress; these might be annually or might be at points in the year such as the Easter holidays, first day back in September, whatever dates work for your vision and plan.

For each date write a short list, description or story of what would be happening at that point if you are on track; this is like a mini-vision to make sure you are getting to your destination.

GOING THE DISTANCE

Keep your vision alive

If you tell people clearly where you are going you stand a good chance of getting there. Your vision story creates a picture of success, which your school is driving towards.

Like in Harry Potter when Dumbledore pulls out a silver memory strand and puts it in the pensive for Harry to step into one of his memories, you're trying to do the same with the future image of your school. Make sure you keep talking about it – use new stories and new examples with both children and adults. At best you need to be talking about your vision in some way every day.

Results and progress towards your vision will help keep it alive and keep the team motivated; that's why celebration is so important. The more your celebrations can refer to your vision and culture the more they will do to cement your direction.

You can expect bumps along the way because this level of change, at whole organisational level, is hard. So if you have invested time communicating your vision and culture to every group in the school and find that some people still don't seem to 'get it' don't be disheartened. As a classroom teacher you would have stated your classroom rules to find that some children still didn't seem to 'get it' and so you would find other ways to help them to understand. In some cases this just might not be the right school, the 'right bus', for them.

Focus on your key driver of success: people

Vision and people go together, the vision tells us where we're going and people make it happen. The ongoing investment in your staff to deliver the vision will turn it into a reality. Investment might mean training but might also mean opportunities. The methods we've covered in this book are all ways to grow and keep growing your team. Your main job as a leader is to develop your people to be the best they can be.

Focusing on your people, spending time thinking about the teams in your school and how best to develop them, having some reflection time - these are all things which are important but not urgent which means they can easily 'drop off' your *To Do* list, or sit forever at the bottom. Be aware of this.

Get new staff up to speed with your culture

Every year you will have new staff, they might join in September or other points throughout the year so take some time to make sure they understand your vision and the culture of your school as quickly as possible. Use those three leadership strategies:

1. Make sure the vision has been shared with them, tell them stories of what has been happening in your school which typifies what you're working to create.

2. Give them some constructive feedback early on. It's likely there will be a honeymoon period and then the storming will begin, the sooner you can establish

a relationship with feedback, ideally two-way, the more likely you are to set up a relationship with healthy conflict. I do this with my team by taking the first opportunity I can to give them useful constructive feedback. This way they know the standards I expect and that our relationship will be one of honesty and feedback.

I also create opportunities for them to give me feedback and I particularly focus on their constructive feedback because people tend to be more nervous about giving this and I want them to know I welcome it. You can see giving feedback as a way of training and explaining your school culture.

3. Look for what their strengths are and help them to develop them as well as any areas you or they feel need to improve. Invest in them and show you're committed to their excellence.

When people move into a new school they are soaking up information about what is and isn't acceptable and so the culture you have established, the consistency with which it is applied and how a new team member is treated are all important in helping them understand, fit in and deliver in your school.

Keep your radar up

You and your senior leaders will need to keep a constant eye on your culture. If there is an issue that arises then deal with it quickly, like the teacher at my first school said 'I pick up on the small things so the big things don't happen'. If you are in doubt, sort it out.

Any violations of your school culture need to be tackled well **because behaviour breeds behaviour and you need the best behaviour, adult and child, across your school if you are to create the school you want to lead.**

You are on a mission to create amazing education by creating a high performing culture. You will need to give great feedback and deal with difficult situations, you will also need to protect your team from any behaviours that will damage the culture you are creating, all while you move toward your vision.

It's hard work but I don't think you became a Head for an easy life or to be average. I think you want to make the biggest positive difference you can to the lives of others.

CHAPTER SUMMARY

- *Keep talking about your vision*
- *Spend time with new staff making sure they understand your culture*
- *Remember culture is a long game so be consistent and stick with it*

Good luck

I hope that you have found this book useful. I've tried to share the best of the best of the work I use in schools in these pages. Most of all I hope you use it to raise the performance of your school even higher, to the vision you had when you became a head teacher.

Being a head teacher is a demanding role. I see that every day but it is, in my opinion, the most important leadership role in any society because you are leading the development of our next generation, the ones who will be running the country 30 years from now. For this I have tremendous respect for you.

Focus on the three key strategies of leadership and apply them consistently to move your leadership and school culture to a higher level. I hope you create the school you have always dreamt of leading and that you have enjoyed the journey to get you where are today and enjoy the exciting journey that lies ahead.

Thank you and good luck.

References

Bass, B. M. (2008). *Transformational Leadership.* Mahwah, New Jersey: Lawrence Erlbaum Associates Inc.

Berne, E. (1964). *Games people play.* New York: Grove Press.

Collins, J. (2001). From *Good to Great: Why Some Companies Make the Leap... and Others Don't.*

Department for Education (UK) (2013). Teacher Standards. Retrieved April 10th, 2014, from www.gov.uk: *https://www.gov.uk/government/publications/teachers-standards*

Kahneman, D. (2011). *Thinking, Fast and Slow.* London: Penguin Books.

MacLean, P. (1990). *The Triune Brain in Evolution: Role in Paleocerebral Functions.* New York: Plenum Press.

Mehrabian, A. (1981). *Silent messages: Implicit communication of emotions and attitudes.* Belmont, CA: Wadsworth.

Ofsted inspection report, Miles Coverdale, 2013. (n.d.). Ofsted inspection report, Miles Coverdale. Retrieved August 7th, 2014, from Ofsted: *http://www.ofsted.gov.uk/inspection-reports/find-inspection-report/provider/ELS/100326*

Ofsted inspection report, St George the Martyr, 2013. (n.d.). Ofsted inspection report, St George the Martyr.

Retrieved August 7th, 2014, from Ofsted:
*http://www.ofsted.gov.uk/inspection-reports/find-inspection-report/
provider/ELS/100040*

Ofsted inspection report, Woodmansterne 2013. (n.d.).
Ofsted Woodmansterne report. Retrieved August 7th, 2014,
from Ofsted:
*http://www.ofsted.gov.uk/inspection-reports/find-inspection-report/
provider/ELS/100590*

Peters, D. S. (2011). *The Chimp Paradox: The Mind
Management Programme for Confidence Success
and Happiness*. Croydon: Vermilion.

Rath, T. (2007). *Strengths Finder 2.0*. New York: Gallup Press.

Tuckman, B. (1965). *'Developmental sequence in small
groups'.* Psychological Bulletin, 63, , 384-399.

Whitmore, J. (1992). *Coaching for Performance*. London:
Nichola Brealey.

Whitmore, J. (2002). *Coaching For Performance: Growing
People, Performance and Purpose*. Finland: Nicholas Brealey
Publishing.

Figures

Index

About the author

Sonia Gill is the Director of *Heads Up Limited*. She studied psychology, is a qualified teacher and entered the business world by being selected to join the *John Lewis* graduate leadership programme. Her experience and success in business coupled with her desire to return to education led to the creation of *Heads Up*.

She realised school leaders were not always well supported or trained in core leadership skills, especially those required to create high performing teams and cultures of excellence. Yet what so many of them did, as class teachers, was exactly that and her ability to translate the skills of a classroom teacher to those of leadership and culture creation make her work very accessible to school leaders. All who have experienced working with *Heads Up* recommend them. Through cultural development programmes, conferences, training and coaching, she and her team support school leaders create outstanding school cultures.

Her belief is that every school can be outstanding and her mission is to make that a reality.

Journey to Outstanding cultural development course

If you're interested in our *'Journey to Outstanding'* courses, which equip school leadership teams with the skills to create a lasting and culture of excellence you can take a look at what these courses 'typically' look like at:
http://www.ukheadsup.com/our-services/journey-to-out-standing-senior/

Why do I say 'typically'? Well we know that your school is unique, so we tailor our courses to what is right for you. On our website we show you what works in most schools but we know *one size doesn't always fit all.*

Free online resources

Find out more about three leadership strategies with our free resources at: *http://www.ukheadsup.com/*

Meet recently outstanding Heads

If you want to learn the best practice from recently Outstanding Heads you can see their presentations at: *http://www.ukheadsup.com/outstanding-heads-best-practice/*

Annual Conference

Come along to our annual conference *Moving to outstanding – best practice from recently outstanding head teachers'* where you will hear from great Heads and meet many others who are striving for excellence (make sure you register your interest in attending the conference because it sells out quickly every year!).

How to Contact Heads Up

We would love to hear from you so feel free to email, post or call at:

www.ukheadsup.com
info@ukheadsup.com

Kemp House
152-160 City Road London
EC1V 2NX

+44 (0) 7973 769 678

Lightning Source UK Ltd.
Milton Keynes UK
UKOW07f1605260115

245141UK00001BA/1/P